MW00510968

Welcome to the team.
Enjoy the Journey !

Gary Weuve

CLOSE MORE SALES IN FINANCIAL INSTITUTIONS

12 KEYS TO SUCCESS

GARY WEUVE

THE BUSINESS INSTITUTE
Manhattan Beach, California

Closing More Sales in Financial Institutions: 12 Keys to Success

Copyright © 2012 by The Business Institute. All Rights Reserved.

No part of this book may be reproduced or transmitted in any form or by any means, electronic or mechanical, including photocopying, recording, or by any information storage and retrieval system, without permission from the publisher.

For information about this title or to order other books and/or electronic media, contact the publisher:
The Business Institute
952 Manhattan Beach Blvd., Ste 200, Manhattan Beach, CA 90266
paul@paulkarasik.com

This publication consists solely of the author's opinions, is not the opinion of any company with which the author may be affiliated, and is designed to provide accurate and authoritative information. It is sold with the understanding that neither the publisher nor the author is engaged in rendering legal, tax, accounting, investment, or other professional service. If legal, tax advice, or other professional services are required, the reader should seek the services of a qualified professional for legal, tax, accounting, investment-planning, and other advice. Before implementing any practice management processes, first check with your broker-dealer's compliance department. The author and publisher cannot be held responsible for any loss incurred as a result of specific investments or business planning decisions made by the reader.

Website: www.centerforadvisorexcellence.com
gary@garyweuve.com

LCCN: 2012937722
ISBN: 978-1-4507-9988-1

Cover Design: Frank Lacey
Editing: Michelle Hutchinson
Interior Design: 1106 Design

Printed in the United States of America
First edition
10 9 8 7 6 5 4 3 2 1

DEDICATION

To my three favorite little people, my grandchildren: Ashton, Addyson, and Aaden

CONTENTS

FOREWORD

ANYONE WHO HAS SERVED in the armed forces knows that an outstanding military leader accomplishes the assigned missions and takes great care of the troops. Both tasks are vitally important to the overall success of the organization. Toward that end, the military spends a great deal of time training its officers on effective leadership skills, particularly as they are applied in the field.

During my time in the military, I observed several different leadership styles, but as a group, I could divide military leaders into two categories: those who thought they knew what their soldiers needed and those who definitely knew what their soldiers needed.

The latter would spend time with their troops, ask questions, listen to answers, and contemplate the responses. Because of their empathetic leadership style, these officers had a good sense of what equipment, strategies, or additional manpower would help the soldiers accomplish a task.

Though Gary does not come from a military background, shortly after I met him, I put Gary in that group of empathetic leaders. We were coaching a young, forward-thinking sales manager in Florida who was interested in building a team of world-class, institution-based financial advisors for his broker-dealer.

While we worked with this particular individual, I watched Gary listen to the manager describe his vision for the unit. As a result, Gary gained a keen understanding for what was required to fulfill the goals the manager had set for the group. Gary designed and then delivered a series of workshops and coaching sessions for the advisors so they could hit the sales manager's mark. In a short period of time, this group of advisors was one of the broker-dealer's top-performing teams.

Now, years later, Gary has gathered his field-tested ideas, tips, techniques, and processes into a book designed to assist any financial advisor or sales manager with building a successful financial services business within a financial institution. Anyone can implement Gary's practical ideas immediately. In twelve chapters, he covers how an advisor or group of advisors can build a branded reputation that will create pull, one that will compel customers to seek out the advisor for his or her expertise and advice.

Gary's practical business-building ideas include marketing concepts for raising awareness of the investment program within the financial institution, methods for gaining a consistent flow of referrals from staff and clients, and strategies for delivering successful workshops like a seasoned public-speaking pro. He shares a winning sales process designed to create not just satisfied customers but loyal clients. Finally, he gives you ideas on how to build a successful business and still maintain a balanced life.

Gary's proven methodologies really work and will lead to success for any financial advisor or sales manager.

Colonel Brian Warren
U.S. Army, Retired
Principal, Partners for Performance

INTRODUCTION

"Most successful men have not achieved their distinction by having some new talent or opportunity presented to them. They have developed the opportunity that was at hand."
—Bruce Barton

IN THE THIRTY-PLUS YEARS I have been in the financial services business, one difference between successful and struggling financial advisors has always stood out. The outstanding financial advisors took on the responsibility for their success. They didn't wait for their employers to supply them with leads. They didn't wait for the companies they represented to come out with the hottest new product or solution. They viewed themselves as the owner of a financial advisory business and not as an employee of a company.

That is what this book is all about, helping you take charge of your business today by walking you through various assessments, exercises, and assignments to get you on the path to the life you envisioned when you originally chose this career. You might be completely off course in your business right now, or your business might just need a little tweak here and there. In either case, this is the right book for you.

Specifically, this book is for the financial advisor who sits in a financial institution, for this is a unique place. Not only do you need to manage your clients and your team, but you need to manage the relationships of those who work for the financial institution. You need to manage the frontline staff such as the tellers and personal bankers, the personnel in the loan department, and senior management. And what you manage are the attitudes they have about you and what you do for the customers, which, in turn, affect the support the financial institution's representatives have for the investment program. Everyone needs to be onboard, supportive, and engaged.

This book is all about taking time to work *on* your business so that you can be more productive and successful while working *in* your business. Think back over the past year. How much thought have you put into your business's direction and growth opportunities and identifying and finding more of your ideal clients?

You as a Business Owner

Michael Gerber wrote a groundbreaking book called *The E-Myth Revisited* in which he investigated the high failure rate of small businesses. You see, most of us believe that small businesses are started by independently minded, success-driven entrepreneurs, but Gerber found that most small businesses are started by technicians, individuals who are extremely competent in their craft but have little idea of what it means to start, manage, and succeed in a small business.

You are the owner of your own small business, one that provides financial advice to the investing public. Even if you sit in a bank or credit union, it is still your business at which to succeed or fail. As Gerber points out in his book, every small-business owner, including the financial advisor, needs to perform three different roles within his or her business or firm:

- ➤ Entrepreneur
- ➤ Manager
- ➤ Technician

Each has a unique function in your business. For example, the entrepreneur or owner is the visionary who decides the direction of the firm and takes responsibility for the firm's ultimate success. It is the part of you that decides whom you will serve (your ideal client) and what products and services the firm will offer.

The manager makes sure procedures are in place that allow the firm to run smoothly and without mishap and takes responsibility for the design and implementation of various required processes including but not limited to the:

- ➤ Client-acquisition process
- ➤ Sales process
- ➤ Processes for onboarding new clients
- ➤ Client-service processes
- ➤ Staff- and client-relationship processes

When you are in the manager mode, you are responsible for making sure enough marketing and sales activity occurs on a daily, weekly, and monthly basis so that the annual revenue goals you have set for your business are met.

The technician is your role as the financial advisor, the part of you that is turning out, delivering, and implementing the plans for your clients' future financial success. The technician is also responsible for staying current with product enhancements, the global economy, and tax law changes that could affect clients' financial plans. Of course, the most important activities of the advisor are:

- ➤ Prospecting for new clients
- ➤ Meeting people
- ➤ Creating financial plans
- ➤ Gathering assets

As we work through the pages ahead, we will cover time-tested and proven techniques that will allow you to function effectively in each of these roles.

The Balance Wheel of Success for Your Business

As you build your business, you must effectively and consistently execute twelve key strategies to achieve a high level of success. Use the balance wheel of success in figure 1 to rate yourself on each of the individual strategies. A five indicates a high rating while a one indicates a low rating. Be brutally honest. You are establishing a baseline here.

Effective execution of these strategies on a routine basis will get you to the life you envisioned when you first started in this business. Your objective is to eventually rate yourself a five in each of the strategies. You want your "wheel" as big and symmetric as possible. If you currently rank yourself all ones, then you have a symmetric wheel, but it has to turn very fast to get anywhere. In other words, your business isn't very efficient. You have to work many hours to get anywhere. If you have some fives, some threes, and a couple of ones, your business bounces down the road with periods of efficiency and inefficiency.

Figure 1: Balance Wheel of Success

Now that you have ranked yourself and your business in each of the categories, notice the ones where you scored the lowest. Spend more time on the chapters of this book that address those weaknesses. If you scored a five in some of the strategies, you may only want to review the related chapters for new ideas on how to fine-tune your business strategy.

As you work through this book, imagine that you are building a franchise using business processes that others can replicate for their success.

I am excited that you have found this book. May it provide the path to not only succeed in your business but in your life as well.

Enjoy the journey!

Gary Weuve, CFP®
Registered Corporate Coach™
The Center for Advisor Excellence™

CHAPTER 1

Position Yourself Above the Competition: Branding

"You were born an original. Don't die a copy."
—John Mason

I LIVE IN AUSTIN, the capital of Texas and the Live Music Capital of the World. You can hear any type of music on any given weekend. In fact, Austin hosts two major music festivals a year: South by Southwest in the spring and the Austin City Limits Music Festival in the fall. During each of those events, thousands of music fans from all over the country descend on Austin because of its reputation as a great music city. The city's brand brings them in.

What is it about your practice or business that would cause people to descend on you or seek you out? What is your reputation? What is your brand? These may be questions you have never pondered in relation to your financial services practice, but they are important ones to consider.

Your brand is everything clients or potential clients will see, hear, and feel about you, your team, and your firm. Your brand includes:

➤ Your firm's name and logo
➤ The brochures you use
➤ Your processes
  – Client service
  – Client communication
  – Sales
  – Marketing
  – Client onboarding (including post-sale paperwork)
➤ Workshops you deliver
➤ Client events
➤ The appearance of your office
➤ How the phone is answered (including the voice mail message)
➤ The expertise of you and your staff
➤ How potential new clients are greeted when they first arrive at your office

Everything you do says something about you and your brand. Just look at the iPhone or iPad. Since their introduction, how many other companies have come out with similar products? The differentiating factor, however, is what you experienced when you purchased the product and what happened after you took it out of the box. Did the salesperson seem knowledgeable and demonstrate the product to you? Were you wowed by the utility and functionality? Did the device immediately work when you got home?

Jeff Bezos, the CEO of Amazon.com once said, "It has always seemed to me that your brand is formed, primarily, not by what your company says about itself, but by what the company does." As we have moved to a service-driven economy, this has become even more important. In his book *The Brand Called You,* author Peter Montoya wrote, "[Your personal brand is] a clear, powerful, compelling public image." It sounds like he is talking about your reputation, doesn't it?

Think of it this way: If one of your best clients were approached by a friend or business colleague and asked, "Hey, who do you use for your investment advice, and what can you tell me about him or her?" what would your client's answer be? Is it the response you would want the client to give?

This is one question to which you must know the answer. You have to know how others view you and your business. As best you can, you should control the answer your client would give in the hypothetical situation above. The payoff is having current clients sing your praises so that their friends, family, and co-workers seek you out for information, sage advice, and the solutions to financial problems.

What Does a Personal Brand Do for You?

A personal brand helps clients and potential customers see you as different. Average doesn't sell; different does. In a world where being average is the norm, being different is a benefit. A strong brand identity will provide you with that market differentiation and a reputation of excellence.

Branding also encourages people to want to see you because you have the answers to their questions. Remember, we don't sell products; we sell solutions to financial problems. A well-designed and well-executed brand strategy will allow your name and reputation to precede you.

By the way, branding yourself and your business really isn't an option. You already have a brand; everyone does. Your brand today is either attracting new clients or pushing them away. What I am suggesting here is that you take control of your brand and not leave it to chance. Your brand is an important element of your business success.

What Is the Value of a Branding Strategy?

What price would you pay to have a dominant position in the market? What is the value of a great reputation? The time invested in planning and executing a personal brand strategy is well worth the effort.

The return on investment for your branding efforts will show itself in many ways. We call this your *branding ROI*. You know you've hit on a successful brand when you are asked to serve on a product or planning committee for your broker-dealer. Your reputation, along with your colleagues' respect for you and your opinion, generates invitations for you to participate.

When potential clients tell you they are bringing their retirement rollovers to you even though the individuals aren't retiring for another two years, you are seeing another sign of success. In his book *The Power of Personal Branding*, Tim O'Brien calls this the "power of pull." You have become the advisor of choice before the money is available.

Your branding ROI will also show itself in the strength of the business you have built. When it will stand the test of time over several market cycles, you know you have built a sustainable business, one that gives you a great deal of career security and stability.

Differentiation

As you begin to think about your brand, focus on differentiation. How are you different from all your competitors? What makes you unique, and does this uniqueness cause people to want to do business with you? Harry Beckwith wrote a book called *What Clients Love*, and in it he said, "…statistics overwhelmingly show that people buy the person first, the company second, products/services third and price last." Clients buy from you because of you.

Today, there are fewer and fewer points of differentiation. You can't differentiate yourself on product; we're all selling the same stuff. You can't differentiate yourself by saying you provide excellent service; everyone says that. So how do you differentiate yourself from the masses?

You might start by asking yourself: How am I unique? How can I differentiate myself in a way that will attract new clients on a consistent basis? The answer lies in a little research. First, check out the websites of your competitors. What are they saying about themselves? What are their marketing positions? Are they all saying the same thing? Do any of the companies or advisors standout from the crowd?

Next, consult your best clients. Invite them out, individually of course, for a cup of coffee, breakfast, or lunch and ask them why they decided to do business with you. What do they like that you do? What is different about you compared to other advisors? Is there something you are not providing that they think you should? The answers to these questions could be the things that make you unique.

What happens, though, if, after conducting all this research, you find out you are just like everyone else: average? Hopefully, that will give you the motivation to create a unique market position. If you don't know how to do that, follow these two steps:

Step 1: Determine how people see you. What is your current brand? I've already mentioned that you need to ask your best clients how they perceive you, but you will also want to use this process with key personnel at the financial institution and potential centers of influence, people who are willing and able to introduce you to ideal prospects and have enough influence so that the introduction has meaning. Get a broad representation of your current reputation in the market.

Step 2: Conduct a gap analysis to determine the difference(s) between your current brand and your desired brand. Once you have a good sense of how you are being viewed in the market, decide how this matches up against your desired image. Determine where you need to adjust or create new perceptions that will enable you to bridge to your new brand.

Creating a Value Proposition

After you have figured out your unique market position, it's time to create your value proposition. Your value proposition is four or five sentences that explain clearly and concisely why an investor would do business with you. What value do you bring to the relationship? It explains you as the financial advisor, your processes, and why that would matter to the client or prospect.

A value proposition could also lead you to position yourself as one of the following:

- ➤ Retirement Specialist
- ➤ Wealth Manager
- ➤ Financial Planner/CFP®
- ➤ Investment Specialist
- ➤ Estate Planning Specialist
- ➤ Insurance Specialist

Next, decide what you do for your clients and potential clients. For example, if you position yourself as a wealth manager, what does this mean? It means you would not only tackle clients' investment issues but also help them figure out their life insurance and long-term care issues. Keep in mind the work you just completed on your value proposition.

Here's another way to think about it: What will you be known for? Will it be for your expertise or your specialization with a certain type of client? Maybe your sales process is better than anyone else's, or you're a comprehensive financial planner, or your level of communication with clients is second to none.

You might already be providing this or similar support for your clients, but articulating this in a few short sentences will allow your clients to view your offering as unique and will take your market position to a higher level. You are creating a market brand that will cause your clients to stay with you and to talk to others about you. You're building a group of client advocates for you and your business.

Building Brand Equity

Differentiation is strongly tied to brand equity, that is, client commitment to you and your team. Think of brand equity much like you would think about a 401k retirement account. The objective is to make consistent deposits over time and to minimize the withdrawals because, just like with a 401k account, withdrawals come with a penalty.

You open your 401k account with the first deposit. You open your brand equity account with the first interaction you have with a prospect. If the interaction leaves the potential client with a positive feeling, you have made a deposit. If the contact doesn't go so well, then you have made a withdrawal and your account may go in the red.

Your account builds with each positive call, contact, or appointment. If you consistently deliver on the positive experiences, you gain authenticity in the client's mind. This will lead to a feeling of trust and eventually, to loyalty. Loyal clients stay with you through an entire market cycle, and with just a little extra effort, you can turn loyal clients into advocates for you and your business. Essentially, they say to you, "I will give you all my money to manage, and I will introduce you to my family, friends, and co-workers." We'll cover the topic of client advocates in more detail in chapter 6.

The Personal Brand Pledge and the Communication of Your Brand

Now that you have built the brand you wish to deliver, it is time to take the personal brand pledge. This involves three specific promises.

The first promise is delivering on the brand experience you envision. For example, if you say your level of communication with clients is second to none, then you need to make sure you have the infrastructure and repeatable processes to deliver that experience. Give consideration to what additional resources you will require. Should you refine some of your existing processes, build new processes, add technology, or hire additional staff?

The second promise is communicating your branded market position. Your targeted audiences won't know about your branded position in the market if you don't tell them. There are four major groups or targeted audiences to whom you will want to consistently communicate your personal brand message:

➤ Your clients
➤ Your potential clients
➤ Your staff
➤ The staff and management of your financial institution

Continually remind your clients why they chose you as their financial advisor. Their memories are short, so don't fall into the mistaken belief that they will remember. Human beings are selfish. We all know this. It is all about what is in it for them. Use this to your advantage and constantly remind your clients what you are doing for them. When rebranding yourself, communicate your new brand during client reviews. At the end of a meeting, mention that in response to feedback you had solicited from your clients you will be implementing specific changes. Then outline those changes that will affect how you are perceived in the market. Broadcasting your new branding message in this manner also tells your clients that their opinions matter since these changes are a result of direct feedback from them.

Of course, you want to communicate your brand to your *potential* clients too. Make this a part of your overall marketing/communication plan for the year. Review all of your advertising and marketing materials to be sure they are in line with your newly chosen market position. If you have a website, spend time reviewing its content as well. What do these information sources say about you and your program? Are they consistent with your desired brand message?

You will also want to make sure the processes leading to a phenomenal customer experience are in place. As an example, if your brand is that of a comprehensive wealth manager, then your data-gathering process needs to encompass an in-depth and comprehensive review of all aspects of a potential client's financial circumstances. A cursory review of his or her risk tolerance will not do. Implementing the processes that lead to a phenomenal customer experience will take some effort on your part but will be well worth the investment.

Also think about new channels for communicating your brand to potential clients. Will your new brand position allow you to develop a strategic alliance, a relationship with another professional, such as a tax attorney, whose expertise complements yours? Developing this type of joint venture allows you and the other professional to exchange client referrals.

Next, you need to make sure your own staff understands your brand and what you are trying to accomplish. Do this during one of your weekly team meetings. Remember, your staff members are an extension of you and influence the impressions formed by your clients and potential clients. Helping your staff understand your differentiating factors and the brand you want to convey will enable your team to reinforce your brand with every customer interaction.

You need to communicate your brand to the personal bankers, loan officers, tellers, platform advisors, and other staff of the financial institution too. They should understand why you are a part of the financial institution's product offering as well as what you do for customers. They need to be comfortable with what you represent and know why your work is important to the customers; your brand will help you communicate this message. You will certainly want to discuss with them the steps of your branded sales process. You can do all of this during staff trainings and during impromptu lunchroom conversations.

Like the staff, the institutional management team needs to understand your brand and the value you bring to the customers of the bank or credit union. You also need to remind the managers why they implemented an investment program at the bank and why they chose you as the investment advisor. Focus on your value proposition with this group. Reinforce all of this during your one-on-one performance reviews.

Remember, tell all these groups that the changes being implemented are based on direct customer feedback. Otherwise, you will leave your audiences wondering why you weren't doing this all along.

The third promise of the pledge involves committing to your brand in everything you do inside and outside the financial institution. You can't be one person in the office and someone else outside your work environment. Just ask John Edwards, Michael Phelps, or Tiger Woods. A misstep can wreak havoc on your brand. You have worked hard to create your brand, so pledge to live it 24/7.

Branding Calendar

Once you have created your unique market position and relayed it to others, you must build an implementation calendar.

For example, if you have told your clients that you are going to launch a series of informational webinars on obstacles and opportunities within the current markets, then, over the months ahead, you must schedule these webinars into your calendar so you can deliver on the promised sessions.

Summary

Remember, everyone has a brand. Control your brand; don't leave it to chance. Everything your clients, potential clients, and financial institution personnel see, touch, hear, or experience is part of your brand. Harley-Davidson says, "The secret to our enduring brand lies in delivering an experience rather than just a collection of products and services." Branding begins with the one or two things that differentiate you from your competition.

Build brand equity with your clients. The greater the brand equity, the deeper the relationship you will have and the more valuable the client will become. This value will show up in growth in assets under management and in increasing referrals.

Brands evolve over time. You will want to review your brand on a consistent basis in order to keep it up to date and in line with the desires and wishes of your clients.

➢ **Action Plan**

1. Complete strategic client research interviews with ten of your best clients and five centers of influence. Once you have completed the interviews, review them to determine your current brand. Decide if this is the brand you want. Also, look for your differentiating factor or for something you could use to differentiate your business.

2. After you have reviewed and analyzed the information from your clients and centers of influence, determine the brand you will deliver. What will be your clients' experiences as they work with you?

3. Perform a gap analysis on your brand. As you think about your new vision for your brand, what will it take to deliver on that vision?

4. Now, with your new brand clearly in mind, write your value proposition, the four or five lines that clearly tell people why they should do business with you.

5. Communicate your brand.

6. Develop your brand launch calendar.

7. Now implement!

CHAPTER 2

Create Your Roadmap to Success: Goal Setting and Strategic Planning

*"One of the amazing things we have been given
as humans is the unquenchable desire to have dreams
of a better life, and the ability to establish
goals to live out those dreams."*
—Jim Rohn

Is IT POSSIBLE FOR YOU to be successful and achieve your dreams without planning? Maybe temporarily; if you're willing to put your head down and run hard, you can accomplish certain short-term goals. But in the long run, you will burn out. Sustainable, long-term success requires a well-thought-out, executable plan.

So how do you begin? Mark Twain said, "The secret of getting ahead is getting started. The secret of getting started is breaking your complex overwhelming tasks into small manageable tasks, and then starting on the first one." That's exactly how you need to initiate your plan.

The core elements of any business-planning process include:

1. Goal Setting

2. Visioning

3. Performing a SWOT Analysis

4. Writing a Strategic Plan

5. Developing Tactics

6. Formulating Timelines

7. Budgeting

8. Monitoring

9. Maintaining Self-Motivation

The development of each of these core elements can become your manageable tasks. As we work together through the process, I will cover each of these elements in more detail.

Goal Setting

Goal setting is used by just about every financial advisor. In fact, every year, I imagine your manager comes to you asking for your annual production goals. If you are like most, you give him or her a production number, and that's the last time you think about it for the year. But if you would give this process a little extra thought and attention, imagine the impact goal setting could have not only on your business but your life.

As an example of how goal setting works, let's look at a friend who likes to run and participate in endurance races. When I asked him why, he said he likes the atmosphere around the events, he likes running with others, and he likes challenging himself. When he races, he wants to be competitive within his age group. To accomplish this objective, he has to put a training plan in place.

When he decided to run his first marathon, he didn't roll out of bed the morning of the race and say to himself, "I think I'll run a marathon today." He could have tried, but it's unlikely that he would have finished the race. Instead, he set the objective of running a marathon and then researched races until he found one that was three months away so he could design a training plan and prepare.

The same is true in your business. You don't wake up on January 1 and say to yourself, "I think I'm going to be a million-dollar producer this year." If you decide to become a million-dollar producer, you must make that decision early in the previous year so that you have time to put your plan in place and are ready to implement it on the first day of the new year. You take time to develop a plan.

The goals you develop should be SMART: **s**pecific, **m**easurable, **a**chievable, **r**elevant, and **t**ime-based. As you think about each of these areas, here are some self-probing questions that exemplify the SMART approach:

Specific

➤ Are my goals well defined and understandable?
➤ Could I easily explain them to anyone not in my business?

Measurable

➤ Are my goals ones for which I can easily track results?
➤ Am I able to track my progress from start to finish?

Achievable

➤ Do I truly believe that I can obtain the goals?
➤ Do others I trust believe my goals are achievable as well?

Relevant

> ➤ Do I have the needed resources to accomplish the goals?
> ➤ Why are these goals significant?

Time-based

> ➤ Do I have enough time to achieve the goals?
> ➤ Is the timeframe short enough to maintain enthusiasm?

Visioning

As you begin the goal-setting process, you can use a technique called visioning, that is, picturing the steps to your reaching your objective. As an example, let's go back to my friend the runner. He uses visioning as he prepares for a race. He imagines himself arriving at the starting line: fit, rested, and prepared. He thinks about how he will feel as he passes each of the mile markers, especially the last few, and in his mind, he sees himself crossing the finish line within the time he set as his goal.

In your case, it works like this. If your goal is becoming a million-dollar producer, picture how many clients you must serve and what they look like. Imagine what your income will be on that million dollars worth of production. Think about what you'll do outside of your business that will give you fulfillment. Visualize where you will go on vacation. See your office organization in your mind. These are all good factors to envision, and I'm sure you can think of several more.

Start by imagining the future of your dreams. Write down what you want to achieve. Don't worry about spelling or being grammatically correct, just write. At this point you are trying to capture ideas, thoughts, and concepts. You can always organize the information later.

By using this free-flowing exercise, you will create the goals required to achieve the vision. Think about the short-term or one-year goals and the longer-term five-year goals. In the book *Good to Great: Why Some Companies Make the Leap…and Others Don't*, author Jim Collins says that you also want to think about your BHAGs (Big Hairy Audacious Goals). This is an ultimate ten- to thirty-year goal you have for your business; it defines what you want to build. Your BHAG is a crisp, compelling, easy-to-understand goal that will push you today and keep you focused. That's a great concept!

Performing a SWOT Analysis

The next step in the business-planning process involves an assessment of your current situation; for this, we will use a SWOT (strengths, weaknesses, opportunities, threats) analysis. A SWOT analysis (figure 2) will provide the information you need to reach the desired state you uncovered during the visioning exercise. Let's take a closer look at the four elements of the analysis.

Figure 2: SWOT Analysis

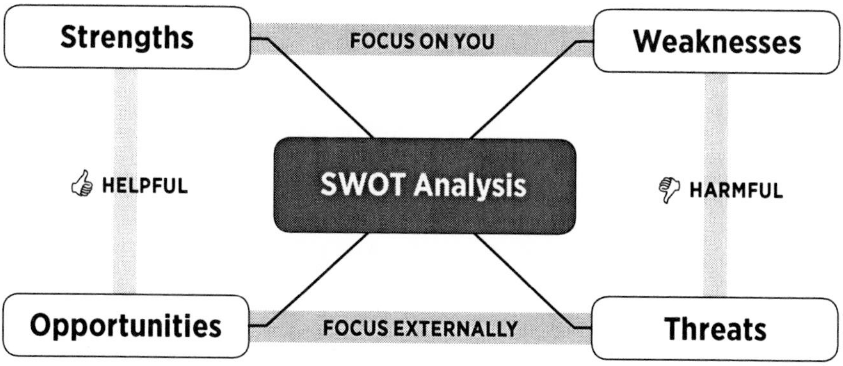

Strengths could include personal characteristics that make you the advisor of choice, the outstanding quality and training of your staff, the dominant position of your financial institution in the market, the financial institution's position as a niche player, or your particular way of doing business that is unique to the industry.

Weaknesses are personal deficiencies. Are you deficient in your education? Are you understaffed or is your staff new and inexperienced? Are you in need of a solid, executable business plan? Do you lack the support of your financial institution?

Opportunities are favorable circumstances. Has a major layoff, downsizing, or early-out program occurred in your community that could lead to rollovers coming your way? Have you recently developed an important and significant center of influence? Have you added new products to your offerings such as corporate retirement plans or long-term care insurance?

Threats are potential risks that could derail your success. Is there a potential for or has there been a recent change in a tax law or legislative policy? Has a new competitor built a new branch right across the street? Is the current economic outlook looking dismal?

Working through the SWOT analysis is necessary because, as you will see, many of the subsequent steps in the planning process are derived from this exercise. Here's how it works.

> ➤ First, list all your personal strengths. Then think about how these listed strengths could be used to enhance your branding message. Are there some points of differentiation here?
> ➤ Then list your weakness. Be brutally honest. This is for your benefit only. Can you improve on or sufficiently manage each listed weakness?
> ➤ Next, give consideration to the external threats to your business. As you list each threat, think about whether or not you can turn that threat into an opportunity.

➤ Finally, list your opportunities. In addition, see if any of your strengths can lead to opportunities and list those too. For example, if you are a terrific public speaker (strength), you may be able to leverage that talent into a guest appearance on a local radio talk show (opportunity). Think about what you can do to exploit and profit from each opportunity listed. This is the fun part of the exercise. We will be turning these into strategic and specific tactical plans later in the process.

Writing a Strategic Plan

Most advisors I talk to know they need a strategic plan. They don't have one because they are overwhelmed by the thought of taking time out of very active and busy business and personal schedules to work on one.

However, writing a strategic plan doesn't need to be a chore. There is a NASCAR adage that says you actually need to slow down to go faster. Intuitively, that does not make a lot of sense, but if you are a NASCAR fan, you know exactly what I am talking about. When a driver goes into the corner too fast, he has to use the brakes to avoid crashing into the wall. The loss of momentum forces him to waste a lot of time and gas to come back up to speed once he exits the corner. However, if he were to lightly let off the gas as he entered the corner and roll through the turn while smoothly applying the accelerator on exit, he would actually go faster.

What I would like you to do is lightly lift your foot from the business accelerator to give yourself time for some strategic planning. Slowing down to develop and execute a strategic plan will actually increase your chances of success. In fact, the bigger the goals, the greater the role a strategic plan will play in the triumphant accomplishment of those goals.

What exactly is strategic planning? It is the art of bringing clarity to your personal and professional goals, identifying the barriers to your goals, and mapping out a plan for overcoming those barriers. The earlier visioning assignment will assist you in defining your desired state, the SWOT analysis will crystallize your present state, and the strategic plan will help you bridge the two. (See figure 3.) As you will see, it is more than simply deciding on a production goal and plotting out a marketing plan.

Figure 3: Strategic Plan – The Bridge from Present State to Desired State

A strategic plan is a series of road maps, each one plotted to accomplish a specific goal or series of goals and get you closer to your desired state. Strategy answers the question, "What should I be doing in my business to achieve my objectives?" or "What broad actions or concepts do I need to incorporate into my business and personal life to accomplish the identified goals?"

Under each strategy, or road map, are tactics, the specific action steps you will incorporate into the strategy. Let's use an example to delve into strategies more deeply here; we will explore tactics in the next section.

Suppose you have a personal goal of working fewer hours in your business in order to spend more quality time with your family without sacrificing income. Additionally, from a business standpoint, you would like to serve a clientele of 200 engaged clients, clients who have given you all their assets to manage and regularly introduce you to others like them. One strategy you could use to reach this goal is a client advocacy program, a program in which you provide your best clients with more personalized customer service and communication. (We will cover client advocacy programs in more depth in chapter 6.)

Another strategy to consider at the same time is moving your best or engaged clients from a transactional model to a fee-based model. This would then allow you to enjoy a more advisory relationship with your best clients while leveling out the revenues to your business. There could be several other strategies that would be appropriate for these combined personal and business goals.

Developing Tactics

Now that you have set your strategies, your next step is to develop your tactics. Tactics are the specific activities or action plans that you build around the strategies. For example, in our previous example of implementing a client advocacy program, some tactics could include:

> ➤ Segmenting your client base into As (top clients), Bs, and Cs (less desirable clients)
> ➤ Identifying the Bs that can become As
> ➤ Reassigning the C clients to a junior advisor
> ➤ Outlining the level of service you will deliver to each segment of your client base
> ➤ Developing a process for nurturing A and B clients through client events

Formulating Timelines

For your overall business plan to be successful, you must develop timelines for achieving each strategy's tactics. The temptation when developing timelines is to offer the most optimistic picture possible, not necessarily the most realistic. Your timelines need to reflect your capacity to accomplish the set tactics or action plans. However, even with careful planning, there will be incidents that may arise that you couldn't possibly consider or imagine such as the September 11 tragedy, Hurricane Katrina, or a real estate meltdown. These unforeseen events may create the need for you to implement a plan B with adjustments to your timelines.

As you are working through the timelines of your various strategies and tactics, remember that some of the activities may be dependent on accomplishing other activities first. For example, it wouldn't be a good idea to plan a client event until you had segmented your client base. Dependent activities need to be completed in a sensible sequence.

Budgeting

Some of your strategies, like sponsoring an event for your best clients, will require a financial investment. There may be expenses for invitations, a caterer, room rental, and gifts. A budget will allow you to link your strategies to the available financial resources. Also, as you budget, remember to prioritize your spending to match the goals you laid out earlier. For example, sticking with the scenario of turning your best clients into engaged clients, you would find it more beneficial to invest resources in existing clients than in trying to find new ones.

Following, is a three-step process you can use for working out a budget.

Step 1: Preliminary budget work. Begin by reviewing your goals, strategies, and tactics. Think about the associated expenses at each level. Then develop simple budgets outlining expected costs. At this stage, it is a little better to overshoot than to skimp.

Step 2: Budget development. Combine the proposed budgets into a single budget listing all of your proposed action plans. In some cases, the total amount needed to execute all your proposed plans will be greater than the monetary amount available to your business.

Step 3: Budget finalization. You may now need to prioritize your spending. Go through the budget line by line with an eye toward your ultimate goals. Consider why one activity is more valuable than another. Of course, you will want to focus on those items with the largest potential financial payoff and the ones that are aligned with your objectives.

Once the budget is built, you will need to find the financing. This can come from three sources: the financial institution, your product partners, and you. Having this framework in hand will help you as you have financial-support discussions with the managers of the financial institution and product partners.

When you commit to this process, you will have a more accurate and practical view of the financial side of your business. Of course, you will want to review your actual expenditures against the budgeted amounts on a monthly basis.

Monitoring

Most advisors I've worked with over the years review their results on an annual basis. At the end of each year, they assess how they did against the objectives they set for themselves. This once-a-year review cycle makes it difficult to manage the execution of the business plan they set up at the beginning of the year. It's crucial that you review results at least quarterly. Ideally, you should monitor results monthly and, for some of your key measures, weekly.

What you will review is dependent on your objectives. I suggest focusing on the key measures from your strategic plan. As an example, if you have a production goal, then reviewing your sales and marketing activities will be important. Are you opening enough new accounts every week? Are you getting a sufficient number of referrals? Are your workshops drawing an adequate number of attendees, and are you converting them to first appointments? Making sure you select the right key measures is very important.

I encourage you to include all of the members of your team in the review process, which need not take a great deal of time. By involving them, you increase their buy-in to the plan and to your business. Here are the steps in the review process.

Step 1: See how you did. Take time to examine and assess the results for each of the key measures established in your strategic plan.

Step 2: Examine the current environment. Re-evaluate your SWOT analysis. Have any new opportunities or threats emerged? Are you able to successfully capitalize on your identified strengths, and have you improved on or properly managed any weaknesses?

Step 3: If you didn't hit plan for the period, or conversely, if the team blew past the goals set, assess why that happened. If performance was below plan, develop activities to get back on track. If you are consistently exceeding your goals, consider why. Was there something significant happening that is repeatable on an ongoing basis, or have you just set your goals too low?

Your end-of-the-year review will be much more in-depth than this. Start with an honest evaluation of your current condition going into the new year. Did you add enough of the right type of new clients during the year? By how much were you able to increase assets under management? Were any new strategic alliances forged? In other words, are you making progress toward the business you initially envisoned?

Maintaining Self-Motivation

What was it that first attracted you to the financial services business? Was it the freedom that comes from running your own business? Self-employment has become the gold standard of dreams for many. I believe it is the freedom and the ability to control your own destiny that attracts many to our business. Sure, you've got the independence of not punching a time clock and have no limitations on your earning capacity, but all of this comes at a price. Running a successful financial services business requires commitment, passion, lots of elbow grease, and above all, plenty of self-motivation. After all, it is up to you, the self-employed owner of a financial services business, to accomplish the objectives you have set for yourself.

So how do you sustain your day-to-day intensity and self-motivation? It helps if you have a system that is part of your overall strategic plan. Here are six important elements of a self-motivation system:

1. Continually review your goals. To get motivated, you need to stay focused on what you're aiming to achieve. Review your goals constantly. Remember my running friend I spoke of earlier in this chapter? He told me one of the reasons he entered races was to improve his motivation for running. It would have been really easy to hit the snooze button on those early mornings when he was feeling a little sluggish or the weather wasn't cooperating, but since he knew he had a race coming up, ego would get him out of bed and on that training run. He'd remind himself of the finish time he had set as a goal, and he wasn't about to let lack of preparation be an excuse for not achieving his desired result.

2. Tell somebody else (maybe your significant other) about your goals and dreams. Communicating them to someone who is important to you makes you more committed to your goals.

3. Don't let your thoughts control your feelings. Understand that thoughts are just that, thoughts. You can choose to accept or reject them. When thoughts of doubt arise, recognize them for what they are, signals that it's time for a little self-motivation boost.

Also, be careful what you listen to, read about, or watch on TV. Certainly gather enough information so that you are aware of what is happening in the world, particularly economically— your clients expect this of you—but don't become a news junkie.

4. Stop procrastinating. One of the biggest killers of motivation is procrastination. Procrastination can come from feeling overwhelmed or just not knowing where to start. Procrastination stymies your activity because the longer you put off a task, the more difficult it is for you to get the ball rolling.

I've heard it said that to be successful, you need to "plan each day a day in advance." That seems to me to be a simple but effective time-management technique. Before you leave the office each day, write down everything you must accomplish the following day, kind of a to-do list. Then prioritize the tasks.

When you arrive at the office the next morning, your tasks for the day are ready for you to tackle.

5. Reward yourself. Now comes the fun part, picking a reward for yourself when you accomplish your goals. Your self-motivation will increase significantly if, from time to time, you give yourself a high-five. Be sure to enjoy the fruits of your labor and a job well done.

Take an afternoon trip to the park with the kids, or make it a movie night with your significant other. For more noteworthy goals, increase the reward, maybe take a weekend getaway.

6. Have fun! Running a financial services practice can be incredibly hard and challenging, but it doesn't have to be unpleasant. Enjoy the career you have chosen. Appreciate the positive impact you have in assisting others in the achievement of their financial dreams.

One way to assure you are having fun is to focus on the type of client you enjoy working with the most. If you're a person who loathes detail, then working with engineers probably wouldn't be the best choice for you. Identify the clients at the top of your book with whom you most enjoy working, and then put plans in place to get more referrals to those types of prospects.

Summary

Spending time on the goal-setting and strategic-planning activities we just discussed might seem tedious but will provide tremendous benefits, including:

1. The establishment of your marketing and sales strategies for the coming year

2. The creation of a common focus for the team and a sense of motivation and ownership

3. The ability to focus everyone on the importance of serving your client base

4. The establishment of financial operating goals

5. The basis for a stronger relationship with your best clients

6. Your development of an awareness of your business's potential in light of its strengths, weaknesses, opportunities, and threats

7. Acceleration and improvement in growth

8. The ability to gain control of operational processes

9. The creation of a definition for success

As you can see, the benefits are numerous, and the process is a well-spent investment in your business.

➤ Action Plan

1. Establish your SMART goals.

2. Complete the visioning exercise.

3. Conduct a SWOT analysis on your current business.

4. Build your strategies and action plans for each goal.

5. Establish the timelines for each goal, strategy, and tactic.

6. Complete your business budget.

7. Monitor your progress toward your goals.

8. Implement the elements of the self-motivation system if necessary.

CHAPTER 3

Generate a Flow of Qualified Prospects: Marketing

"He who has a thing to sell and goes and whispers in a well is not so apt to get the dollars as he who climbs a tree and hollers."
—Unknown

DOORWAYS LEAD US from one place to the next. They can also provide entry to new relationships. Isn't that what marketing is about, opening doors in order to build new business relationships?

Regardless of the size or maturity of your business, attracting new clients is one of the most important activities you perform. If your business is still in the building stage, you need to grow that business as quickly as possible. If, on the other hand, your business is more developed, your needs are different. You are going to lose clients every year due to various factors such as competition, relocations, and death. Those lost clients will need to be replaced, or over time, your business will disappear.

But the challenge in today's financial services marketplace is in getting prospects to hear your marketing message. They have become desensitized to any type of ad or campaign. They are like people walking around all day with remote controls in their hands; the minute they see a marketing message that doesn't convey a perceived immediate need, they change the channel.

You also have a problem getting through to new prospects because of what I call the *crisis of trust* that has resulted from major market meltdowns, Wall Street scandals, and several major Ponzi schemes played out in the broadcast and print media. Investors aren't sure they can trust you.

And then you have the Dodd-Frank Act. If the investing public didn't need protection from investment firms, why would Congress pass this bill? The perception is that we're part of Wall Street and not part of Main Street, so you have much to overcome in the minds of the investing public.

However, most advisors' marketing plans look like the mating ritual of the male Victoria's Riflebird who, during the mating season, performs an elaborate courtship dance by perching alone on a tree stump, stretching his wings outward, bobbing his head from side to side, and calling loudly to potential mates. This *look-at-me, look-at-me* ritual is all orchestrated to attract the attention of a female.

Isn't it much the same with most of the marketing we see from financial services firms? They go through all these elaborate gyrations called marketing with the intent of attracting the attention of an interested investor. Our dance includes a series of posters, seminars, mailings, and hopefully, a client introduction or two. If successful, we end up with a new prospect and potentially a new client.

I want you to rethink your approach to marketing your business, and I want you to understand exactly what you should be marketing. First, remember you provide solutions to financial problems; you are not just selling products. Products are only the means for solving the problems. I'm sure you've heard it said many times—when someone buys a drill, he really isn't buying a drill; he is buying the hole the drill creates. Similarly, when someone buys one of your products, he isn't really buying, let's say, an annuity; he is buying the stream of income the annuity generates.

Second, you are marketing awareness of your business. It is hard to sell when you can't be seen. Customers of your financial institution need to know you exist and how to contact you.

And finally, you need to market your knowledge and skills, the experience and wisdom you've acquired over the years that when applied, help investors solve their complicated financial issues.

I also want you to remember that results will be dependent on the methods used and the execution of the chosen marketing technique. The graph in figure 4 illustrates the effectiveness of various marketing methods and is based on my experience with them. Low-impact methods are on the left; progressively higher-impact methods are encountered as you ascend to the right.

Realize that the methods on the right side of the graph have a greater impact because they enable you to build a relationship of trust far more quickly. Potential investors will respond best to you when they have met you through a friend, family member, or colleague who speaks highly of you and your services. Because of the relationship you have with existing clients, trust is partially transferred to a prospect when a client introduces you. By starting with marketing methods farther to the right on the graph, you're initiating the new relationship at a higher level of trust.

Figure 4: Effectiveness of Marketing Methods

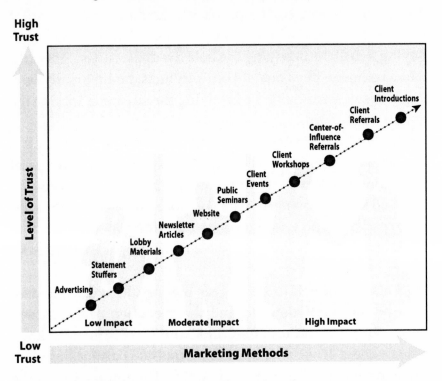

Potential clients can have their investment needs fulfilled at their financial institutions, online, or by stockbrokers, independent advisors, or financial planners. All of these financial suitors are able and willing to assist. However, more than anything, people are looking for someone they can trust to work in their best interest. The methods on the right half of the graph get you to the position of trust more quickly.

In addition, remember that everything you do is marketing. Think beyond the traditional sense of marketing. In every client meeting, every workshop you deliver, and in every article you write, you are marketing your business. Marketing even includes the way your office looks because investors will form an initial opinion about you based on the appearance of your workplace.

And just like you, everyone who touches your business on your behalf is marketing your business. You want to be sure that each interaction is a positive experience. For example, if you are having a guest speaker share some of the face time at one of your workshops, you will want to work with that person ahead of time to make sure she has a message that will resonate with the audience and that she is an accomplished speaker.

Attention to detail is important in marketing; it even comes down to how the phone is answered in your office. Always be asking: How can we make a great first impression every time? Not just the first time, but every time.

From the branding work you did earlier, your overall marketing message is that you stand out, that you are exceptional, that you are not just average. Indifference is everywhere, so with just a little effort and focus, standing out is easy. You've developed your brand, and marketing helps you get your brand message out to the financial institution's customers.

Marketing starts with a written plan. This plan will then become a part of the overall strategic plan we discussed in the previous chapter. The elements of any successful marketing plan include:

- Your value proposition
- Development of a niche
- Strategies with tactics
- Budget and calendar
- Determination of marketing audiences
- Evolving

Let's look at each of these in more depth.

Focus on Your Value Proposition

If I were a competitor reviewing your public marketing information, what would I find? Would I get a sense of what your value proposition is, and would I find it clearly articulated? When was the last time you reviewed your marketing strategies with a critical eye? Is the message being conveyed the one you want your clients and potential clients to internalize?

Your value proposition spotlights the benefits you provide and is communicated in four or five bullet points or sentences or spoken in thirty seconds or less. These statements should be precise and succinct and state why someone should do business with you. Remember, it is not only what you do and how you do it that counts but what benefits the potential clients receive. They want to know what you can do for them.

This message should then be carried throughout your marketing materials, campaigns, and processes. For example, every time you deliver a workshop, you should at some point, either at the beginning or the end, deliver your value proposition.

Development of a Niche

Mass marketing results have fallen off over the last few years. Prospects, particularly high-net-worth prospects, just don't respond to this type of marketing approach. While it can still be successful, it now takes a greater investment of time and money to get the same results. With a little bit of work up front, niche marketing—targeting a specific segment of the population—can provide superior results for your marketing efforts.

Your access to and ability to tap into a niche market might not be readily apparent. You might be thinking that you have a melting pot of clients who represent a broad spectrum of the local population, so you wonder where the niche is in that chaos. If you were to narrow your view of your client base, you would wipe away some of the confusion and bring focus to potential niches.

Here is an exercise I want you to complete. On a sheet of paper, list your top ten clients. Now think about what they have in common. Possibilities include:

- Same age group
- Same employment status (Retired? Still working? If still working, are they near retirement, or are they in the prime of their careers?)
- Same company or similar industry
- Same social or community groups
- Same marital status

As you look through this list of your top clients, you may see other shared characteristics as well. Any similarity is the start of a niche that can be leveraged within your marketing plan.

Also think about your greater neighborhood at large. Is there a dominant employer in the area? What is the region known for, and what businesses support this community image? Does your financial institution cater to a particular type of clientele?

Once you have identified a niche, you need to immerse yourself in the group. You need to familiarize yourself with the members in a way that will allow your reputation to precede you. Being viewed as "one of them" will also improve your level of trustworthiness. Read what the group reads; go where the group goes. That will assist you in understanding the individuals in your chosen niche and their needs. Once you understand the niche market, you can then determine which problems your products and services can solve. Understanding the niche will help you answer questions like:

➤ What is important to the group, and is there some commonality?
➤ What financial issues keep them awake at night?
➤ Why would I be the best financial advisor for the group's members?
➤ When the group works with me, what outcomes will they experience?

Now, I know that because you sit in a financial institution, you may have to work with clients who are outside your niche. Look upon this as the price of admission to your niche group. In addition, a little pro bono work is good for the soul.

Marketing Strategies and Tactics

Your marketing strategies are the broad approaches you will use to inform the members of your identified niche market that you exist and that you are ready to help them with their needs. They should understand the benefit of working with you if your value proposition is part of your overall strategic plan.

Your chosen marketing strategies should saturate your identified niche market or markets. Research shows that the average consumer needs up to five contacts with you, your products, or services to even recognize and remember your name. Therefore, use multiple channels to get the word out.

Here are some potential marketing strategies you will want to consider:

Generating word-of-mouth referrals: The most powerful marketing strategy you will want to use is word-of-mouth referrals. This strategy involves cultivating others to be ambassadors for your business. It means turning your best clients and centers of influence into raging fans so that they tell their family, friends, and co-workers about you and your business. It also involves fostering relationships with strategic alliances. I will talk more about these specific strategies and tactics in the chapters ahead.

Initiating a branch advocacy program: A branch advocacy program is for advisors who serve multiple branches. In this strategy, you appoint an advocate in each of your branches—someone to assist the other branch staff in spotting referral opportunities and remind others of your services. The best advocate is the staff member who, in the past, has been a solid source of referrals. Then, once a quarter, bring all the branch advocates in for recognition and a nice luncheon.

Conducting educational workshops: In educational workshops, you teach your audience members about relevant financial topics—for example, Roth IRAs vs. traditional IRAs, diversification strategies—rather than focusing on products.

Having a virtual footprint: A virtual footprint includes your website as well as your LinkedIn page if your broker-dealer allows you to have one. While a website won't generally drive leads into your business, it will give you legitimacy. Once you have introduced yourself to a potential client, some will want to check you out before they move to the next step. Today's technology allows them to search for you on the worldwide web. If you don't have an Internet presence, you may be limiting your credibility.

Implementing a client communication program: Your clients, particularly your best clients, want to hear from you often. They want to know that you are paying attention, that you are on watch, and that you are monitoring their investments.

Communicate with the top third of your book at least monthly. You should be touching your best clients at a minimum of twice a month, and some would say this should be a weekly occurrence. A touch includes market-update emails or e-newsletters, birthday calls, invitations to workshops and client-appreciation events, portfolio reviews, etc.

Extending your client communication program to prospects: Once you have a solid client communication program in place, extend it to your top prospects. This strategy could work to your advantage from several perspectives. For example, a friend of a client could mention to you that he is hearing about all the information you provide and wishes his advisor were as proactive. Offer to put the client's friend on your communication list. It gives you an opportunity to turn him into a client later on. Or how about a prospect you have met who isn't retiring for another couple of years? Your client communication program would be an excellent way to stay in touch until her retirement plan rollover becomes available.

Developing centers of influence: Besides clients and staff, who else can assist you with referrals and introductions? Think about potential centers of influence. How about the human resources director at a business that has a relationship with your financial institution? If you already have three or four clients from this business, you have a good sense of their fringe benefit program. This insider knowledge allows you to understand precisely how your products and services provide advantages to these employees when they retire.

Use the business's relationship with the financial institution to arrange a breakfast or lunch with the human resources director.

At this meeting, layout the processes and products you use to help the business's employees retire without the fear of running out of money. Let the personnel director know that you also take time to get to know the employees on a personal level as well.

Partnering with a strategic alliance: Forging a strategic alliance with another professional whose expertise complements your business is a great way to get referrals, but remember, in a strategic alliance, to get referrals, you have to give them too. Attorneys, long-term care consultants, and health insurance specialists are great examples of professionals with whom financial advisors can cultivate these types of ventures.

Public speaking: Delivering presentations at various group functions won't necessarily create immediate leads, but it does give your business a market presence. Does your financial institution have a retirees club that meets for lunch once a month or once a quarter? Offer to speak on a topic that would be of interest to them. Seek out other groups too, such as PTAs, the local dental society, etc.

Networking: Be active within the financial institution and in the community. Like public speaking, it gives your business a presence.

Budget and Calendar

Once you have your marketing strategies and their associated tactics in place, your next step is to begin planning your marketing budget and marketing calendar.

Let's start with the budget. Budgeting is simply identifying inflows and outflows, in other words, identifying where the dollars are coming from and how they are going to get spent. You need to maximize the impact your invested marketing dollars will have on finding and attracting new clients.

You could start the budgeting process in a couple of ways. The first is determining the total funds you have available and then spreading those dollars out over the year. The other method involves calculating the total amount you will need for your marketing plan and then looking for the dollars to implement your strategies. Either method will work.

Once the budget is in place, you need to plan your marketing calendar. The easiest way to do this is by quarters. For example, maybe the first quarter will involve an IRA campaign while the last quarter will be a good time for an estate-planning marketing strategy. Also be aware of any campaigns your financial institution might be running; when appropriate, run a parallel campaign.

Who are Your Audiences?

As you think about your marketing plans, you need to focus on your audiences. This will help you determine the best strategies to use for each. The groups you want to target are:

- ➤ Potential clients that meet your niche criteria
- ➤ Clients
- ➤ Strategic alliances
- ➤ Centers of influence
- ➤ Staff at the financial institution
- ➤ Management at the financial institution

We have already discussed potential clients in your niche market, so let's focus on the other groups.

Your clients, particularly your best clients, need to be reminded of what you do for them. They are constantly bombarded with messages from other advisors and firms. People's memories are short and your clients' memories are no different. The client communication program we discussed earlier will be your primary delivery channel for this message.

It takes effort to nurture a strategic alliance and a center of influence. In order for you to stay top of mind with both groups, you need to be in constant contact. Do this by adding both groups to your client communication program and by planning informal get-togethers. Call a strategic partner and invite him out for breakfast, lunch, or a cup of coffee. During this time together, bring him up to date on your business and any changes that may affect future referrals. For example, maybe you are in the process of delivering a series of workshops on social security for your best clients. As you are sharing your plans, suggest that he invite individuals or couples who would be interested in this information.

Don't forget to market to the staff and management at your financial institution too. Just as with your clients, it is important for them to keep you top of mind. They should be just as familiar with your processes and how you assist customers with investment and retirement planning as your clients are. This familiarity will come via staff training, a topic that will be covered in detail in chapter 7. Finally, it wouldn't hurt to remind management why they chose to offer an investment program and why you are the right person for them.

Evolving Your Marketing Plan

Over the years I have noticed that advisors fail to change their marketing strategies, and this causes them to plateau at a particular level of production. Table 1, which is drawn from my own data, shows that advisors who broaden their marketing methods as their careers progress, especially by using client referrals, strategic alliances, centers of influence, and client advocates, tend to generate more revenue. Continuing to rely on referrals from the staff or public marketing campaigns is going to limit your growth opportunities.

**Table 1: Correlation between Production Levels
and Marketing Methods**

Production Level (Revenue)	Marketing Method	Percentage of Time Method Used	Career Stage
Up to $250,000	Staff Referrals	50%	Years 1
	Public Marketing	50%	through 3
$500,000	Workshops	25%	Years 4 and 5
	Client Referrals	50%	
	Staff Referrals	25%	
$750,000	Client Advocates	50%	Years 6
	Client Referrals	25%	through 9
	Workshops	25%	
$1,000,000	Strategic Alliances	10%	10 Years Plus
	Centers of Influence	15%	
	Client Advocates	50%	
	Client Referrals	25%	

Summary

Finding and attracting new clients to your business is critical to your success. In a challenging environment, you must review all your current marketing and client-acquisition processes. Volatile markets, investment scandals, and more government regulations have caused the investing public to view financial advisors with a critical eye. The methods used in the past to grow your book may not work in the future.

➤ **Action Plan**

1. Review the graph showing the effectiveness of marketing methods.

2. Review your value proposition.

3. Complete the niche-marketing exercise discussed in the chapter.

4. Decide what marketing strategies you will use and write them down.

5. Under each strategy, list the tactics you will incorporate.

6. Create a marketing budget.

7. Transfer all your marketing activities to a marketing calendar.

Harness the Power of Presentations: Planning Workshops

"Speech is power: speech is to persuade, to convert, to compel."
—Ralph Waldo Emerson

SOME OF THE MOST successful advisors I know, both inside and outside the financial institution market, have initially built their businesses on workshop marketing. Workshop marketing, also known as seminar marketing, is a great way to get new clients, gather assets that existing clients hold in other accounts not currently under your management, and deepen relationships with your best clients. It also allows you to leverage your time by telling your story once to a room of thirty people, as opposed to telling your story thirty times, one person at a time.

In addition, workshop marketing is an outstanding way to build your presence and increase recognition of the investment program within the bank, savings and loan, or credit union. I have heard more and more advisors over the years mention that prospects have visited their offices with retirement plan rollovers because of a workshop the prospects had attended several years earlier. If you would like your clients and potential clients to view you as a retirement-planning guru, begin building your branding foundation by conducting a series of educational workshops on retirement.

Regardless of your current or desired brand, now is the time to get your workshop marketing plan into high gear because bank customers need your guidance more than ever before. Every year, more and more of the 76 million baby boomers are turning 65, but unfortunately, they are not financially ready for retirement. They are the first generation to retire without a majority of individuals having a traditional, defined-benefit retirement plan. Additionally, they have not been very good savers, and when they did save, they were either too conservative or too aggressive in investing their dollars.

Financial Rewards of Workshop/Seminar Marketing

Before we begin discussing how to deliver an effective workshop, let's spend a little time quantifying the financial rewards. We will try to answer the question: What is the payoff of planning and presenting seminars and conducting follow-up activities?

While not for everyone, seminars can be one of the most effective ways for financial advisors to gather assets. The point of any seminar is to generate multiple, mutually profitable, long-term relationships, relationships that lead to trust. And gaining trust in today's business environment is crucial to your success at accumulating clients and their assets.

Know that a seminar-marketing strategy is not an easy road to navigate and should not be taken without an attitude of commitment. It takes planning and dedication to pull off successfully, but this dedication will pay off. Let's use the formula in table 2 to determine what the annual rewards might be.

Table 2: Annual Seminar Payoff Formula

	Total Seminars You Expect to Deliver		_____
1.	Average Number of Attendees* Required for Successful Seminar		_____
2.	Number of Successful Seminars	×	_____
3.	**Total Attendees** (line 1 × line 2)	=	_____
4.	Appointment-Setting Rate	×	_____
5.	**Total New Appointments** (line 3 × line 4)	=	_____
6.	New-Business Closing Rate	×	_____
7.	**Total Attendees Conducting New Business** (line 5 × line 6)	=	_____
8.	Average GDC per Attendee Conducting New Business	× $	_____
9.	**Total New GDC for the Year** (line 7 × line 8)	= $	_____

*An attendee may be a single individual or a couple attending together.

Let's look at each of the elements of the formula in more depth.

Total Seminars You Expect to Deliver: February through May and September to the middle of November are the peak workshop months. Right now, you should be preparing for the workshops you will deliver in these high-performance months. Set a goal for how many you would like to conduct. Challenge yourself. For example, how about delivering two workshops a week every other week over either the spring or fall workshop season? That would be a total of ten to sixteen workshops. Seem impossible? How do you know until you try?

Average Number of Attendees Required for Successful Seminar: How many attendees, on average, need to be present for you to qualify your seminar as a success? Ten? Fifteen? Twenty? The optimum number of attendees is no more than the number of people with whom you can make eye contact during your presentation.

Also, let's agree on the definition of an attendee. If a single person attends your seminar, he/she would be considered an attendee. In addition, a couple attending together would also be counted as one attendee—whether their assets are held jointly or separately—because couples typically go through the financial-planning process together. Think of your attendees as households or pocketbooks. If an adult brings his or her parents to one of your seminars, then you have two attendees: the adult child (one attendee) and the parents (the second attendee).

Number of Successful Seminars: As much as you would like, not every seminar will be a success. You may have a couple where absolutely no one shows up. That's OK because when you are consistently delivering seminars, you will have success with your fair share.

Total Attendees: The total number of attendees is the [Average Number of Attendees Required for a Successful Seminar] multiplied by the [Number of Successful Seminars]. Some of the attendees may already be your clients; that is OK. Inviting existing clients to your workshops is a great way to capture assets held elsewhere. In addition, a good way to boost attendance is to suggest that your clients invite a friend.

Appointment-Setting Rate: This number represents the percentage of attendees who set appointments with you after the seminar. You can increase the rate by having a strong call to action at the beginning of the workshop and a reminder at the end. Continue to refine your call to action until at least 60 percent of your attendees are scheduling a post-seminar appointment with you. Using a feedback form with a "Check yes for a no-obligation complimentary consultation" option is simple and effective.

Total New Appointments: This number represents *all* the new appointments you set as a result of conducting seminars and is calculated by multiplying [Total Attendees] by [Appointment-Setting Rate]. The more strongly you deliver your call to action, the more appointments you will have during the days and weeks ahead.

New-Business Closing Rate: The New-Business Closing Rate is the percentage of appointment-setters who close new business with you once you have finally had the chance to sit down one-on-one with them. This includes new clients as well as existing clients who transfer assets held elsewhere to you. Based on my observations over the years, most advisors in financial institutions are pretty good at closing new business, even if they only capture a portion of new clients' assets at the beginning of the relationship. The key is getting that initial appointment and conducting it appropriately; seminars can help facilitate that meeting.

Total Attendees Conducting New Business: As already mentioned, in the context of this discussion on seminar marketing, new business can result from existing clients who transfer additional assets to you or it can come from new clients. We count existing clients who transfer assets because meeting with that person after he/she attends your workshop generated revenue for your business. Total Attendees Conducting New Business is calculated by multiplying [Total New Appointments] by [New-Business Closing Rate].

Average GDC per Attendee Conducting New Business: If you open a new relationship or are successful in capturing new assets with an existing client, what do you anticipate as the average gross dealer concession (GDC)? You need to decide or estimate this figure in order to complete the Seminar Payoff Formula.

Total New GDC for the Year: Total New GDC for the Year is the product of [Total Attendees Conducting New Business] and [Average GDC per Attendee Conducting New Business]. Think about the impact this additional GDC will have on your business. Will it push you into a higher payout band? Will this additional GDC help you qualify for an elite conference trip?

Let's plug some numbers into the Seminar Payoff Formula so you can really see how it works (table 3).

Suppose you plan on conducting fourteen seminars per year and that you think twelve of them will be successful because they will yield an average of fifteen attendees per seminar. That will give you a total of 180 attendees.

If your goal for your appointment-setting rate is 60 percent and you achieve that goal, then you will have set appointments with 108 attendees. Furthermore, if you close business with 80 percent of the people with whom you set appointments, you will have captured new business from eighty-six attendees.

If these eighty-six individuals generate an average GDC of $2,400/year, then total GDC for the year will be $206,400. And the first-year GDC is only part of the picture. Consider the value of a new client over the life of the relationship, particularly if you have a strong process for gathering client referrals.

Table 3: Annual Seminar Payoff Formula Example

	Total Seminars You Expect to Deliver		14
1.	Average Number of Attendees* Required for Successful Seminar		15
2.	Number of Successful Seminars	×	12
3.	**Total Attendees** (line 1 × line 2)	=	180
4.	Appointment-Setting Rate	×	60%
5.	**Total New Appointments** (line 3 × line 4)	=	108
6.	New-Business Closing Rate	×	80%
7.	**Total Attendees Conducting New Business** (line 5 × line 6)	=	86
8.	Average GDC per Attendee Conducting New Business	×	$ 2,400
9.	**Total New GDC for the Year** (line 7 × line 8)	=	$206,400

*An attendee may be a single individual or a couple attending together.

The Seminar Payoff Formula is now a way to get senior management at the bank to buy in to your workshop-marketing plan. Having the support of senior management will maximize the success of your workshop-marketing efforts. Make sure, as you plan and begin executing your marketing efforts, that the marketing department also understands that you have the support of the bank leaders.

So what's next? Confucius said, "A journey of a thousand miles begins with a single step." Now, I'm not suggesting that designing and executing a seminar-marketing plan is like a 1,000-mile journey, but I will say that any journey begins with that first step. Use the Seminar Payoff Formula to determine the value workshops have in your business plan. Use that information as motivation to help you stay focused on the end result.

Preparation: A Key Element in the Process

Now that you have determined that workshops will pay off in a big way, the next step is to begin planning the workshops you will deliver over the next few months. Every workshop has three elements: preparation, delivery, and follow-up. Let's start at the beginning with preparation, possibly the most important element of the process. Delivery and follow-up will be covered in the next chapter.

The more workshops you deliver, the easier the planning becomes. You get into a rhythm. There are however, several elements to consider.

Your Audience and Objective: Begin your planning by deciding what type of audience members you'd like to attract and what your objective will be. For example, you might like to attract bank customers nearing retirement to meet your objective of obtaining new clients and capturing retirement asset rollovers. Or you might be thinking about a workshop for your existing clients, with the objective of capturing assets currently held outside your institution. Or maybe you'd like to conduct a seminar for members of your client advocacy program (see chapter 6), with the intent of increasing your flow of referrals.

Topic: Only *after* you have decided on your audience and objective should you choose your topic. The topic must be one that will interest your audience, and it will be different for each of the aforementioned scenarios and objectives. For example, you may already have the retirement plan rollovers of your existing clients, so for this audience, social security would be a better topic than retirement plan rollovers.

Your broker-dealer may also provide you with several workshop topics, but to know which one is best, ask the people with the most insight: your best clients, the bank's branch managers, strategic alliances you have built over the years, and your centers of influence.

Be creative with the title of your workshop. Think of it as a headline. A bank customer probably wouldn't be interested in a workshop entitled "Long-Term Care Insurance." However, one entitled "Insuring Your Retirement Nest Egg" or "Protecting the Goose that Laid the Golden Egg" would surely capture attention.

Content: If you have a choice between an existing workshop and creating your own, use the former. Why spend your precious time trying to come up with material for the workshop when content is available through your broker-dealer, product partners, or seminar vendors? The time saved by not preparing your own material can be better utilized marketing your workshop, training staff, or visiting with clients and prospects. You can also use an existing workshop and add a few tweaks to personalize the presentation.

Finally, make sure the workshop you deliver is educational. This is not the time to be selling. The purpose of your presentation is to disturb and motivate. Disturb the attendees enough to make them understand they have a problem and motivate them enough to come see you.

Workshop Type: Think about how you are going to deliver your message. Will it be via a public seminar to which you invite anyone interested in coming, or will it be more selective, such as one for only your best clients? Are you after a large group, or will the workshop be more intimate and smaller in nature? Smaller workshops are gaining in popularity since it is so much easier to begin the trust-building process in a more intimate setting.

Partners or Sponsor: It might pay to spend some time finding a partner or sponsor for your workshop. A business client of the bank might fit that role. A sponsor can help you promote the event, and his/her endorsement gives you added credibility. Sponsored workshops can also be particularly effective if they are held at the partner's business or location.

Workshop Formats: A workshop takes place anytime two or more clients or potential clients are available for a presentation. Therefore, workshops can take place face to face, over the phone, or via a video conference. They can be delivered as a team or with you as a solo presenter. If you are going to deliver a traditional face-to-face workshop, you will want to focus on a smaller, more intimate audience with the meeting lasting no more than an hour.

If you'll be conducting your seminar via phone or video conference, make sure that all telecommunications equipment is functioning properly well ahead of your event. In addition, make sure all participants receive the call-in phone number or video conference website and pass code several days in advance.

Finally, let me take a moment to contrast a workshop with public speaking. From time to time, you may get invited to address a group such as the members of the local senior center or the local business chamber. While these opportunities are important in promoting the bank and its financial-planning program, these activities will not necessarily generate immediate leads for your products and services.

On the other hand, the objective of a workshop is to deepen the relationship with your best clients or to generate additional assets under management either by acquiring new clients or by capturing other assets of existing clients.

Date and Time: Pull out your calendar and select the date for your seminar by considering the day of the week. Tuesdays and Thursdays are best for evening workshops. Wednesdays work well for daytime events.

If you are targeting near-retirees, then you may need to hold the workshop in the early evening. If the targeted audience is retirees, then you'll want to plan a mid-morning or mid-afternoon workshop. Most retirees are available during the day and dislike driving at night.

I have also been involved in workshops that are held on Saturday mornings. With a compelling topic and appropriate advertising, these can be very successful, especially if your targeted audience consists of professionals. They often use weekends for continuing education. Weekday lunches are also good for professionals and business owners. For all others, a seminar scheduled for six o'clock at night is often ideal. That gives people time to travel to your venue after leaving work.

Location: At this point, you need to start zeroing in on the location for your event. I have already discussed the possibility of holding the workshop at a bank customer's business, but other possible venues include hotels, restaurants, colleges, community centers, country clubs, theaters, or your bank/credit union. Let's examine the pros and cons of each.

Hotel: A hotel should be your last resort as a venue because historically, leaders of financial workshops held at these locations have engaged in bait-and-switch tactics, that is, the workshops have been promoted as planning sessions only to have the focus turn to selling of a product. Consumers have now become wise to this strategy. Workshops at restaurants with the promise of a free meal imply the same thing.

University or Community College: An institution of higher education is an excellent choice since the setting projects a sense that the attendee will learn something.

Community Center: A community center is also an excellent choice, particularly if the workshop is targeted to a larger audience and the marketing was more public in nature. Over the years, I have seen community centers host several successful half-day workshops with multiple speakers covering financial-planning topics.

Country Club: Country clubs can work well, but such venues can send the wrong message to attendees if the intent of your seminar is to capture new clients. Prospects may consciously or unconsciously feel that the location implies that you charge high fees. This is true even if you are marketing to the high-net-worth crowd.

Bank or Credit Union: Your financial institution is the best place to conduct your workshop if you can use a boardroom, conference room, or training room that will accommodate the registrants. This site has one big advantage: the attendees know where the bank, savings and loan, or credit union is located.

Marketing: How you are going to market your workshop? If your workshop topic is broad in nature, such as one on general retirement-planning concepts, or is open to the public, then statement stuffers, lobby posters, and flyers that the staff can hand out are the methods you should use. However, if your workshop topic is narrower, such as "Building a Retirement Income You Can Never Outlive," then your audience would probably encompass retirees and near-retirees, a more specific group, and therefore, your marketing will need to be more focused. In this case, picking up the phone and personally inviting your clients will work well.

As you plan your marketing strategy, be sure to involve the bank's marketing department. These folks can be helpful when thinking through the best methods, and they can enhance your marketing strategies. For example, the public relations specialists may be instrumental in getting an article or ad about your workshop in the bank's newsletter.

You will also want to involve the bank's staff in your marketing efforts by sharing the workshop's topic and content with them. This will help them feel engaged and part of the investment program. As a result, they will be more likely to talk to bank customers about your workshop, especially a public one, and increase attendance.

Marketing is the most important element of the preparation process. If you put all your efforts into rehearsing and delivering a spot-on workshop and no one shows up, what have you accomplished? First make sure you will have "cheeks in the seats," and then polish the presentation.

RSVPs: You will need a system for your attendees to make a reservation and for you or your assistant to confirm the reservations. Does the bank or your broker-dealer have a method available to you to provide online reservations? Does the staff understand how to make a reservation? Once you have set the process, you will want to include it in your marketing material and communicate it to the staff.

Getting attendees to register is an important step because it then allows you and/or your assistant to call respondents the day before the workshop to remind them of the event and to confirm they are attending. In fact, when you call, you can use the following script or tweak it to your situation:

Hello, Mr. Smith. This is [your name] from [financial institution name]. Thank you for registering for tomorrow night's seminar on [general topic of your workshop]. I look forward to seeing you. I'm pleased you are coming because you're going to hear some important information that will help you towards your financial goals. I'm reaching out to you to see if you have any specific topics you'd like covered or questions you'd like answered during the workshop.

Great! Well then, I'll see you tomorrow night.

If your assistant makes the call, the script would change slightly to:

Hello, Mr. Smith. This is [assistant's name] from [financial institution name]. I work with [your name]. Thank you for registering for tomorrow night's seminar on [general topic of your workshop]. We look forward to seeing you. I'm pleased you are coming because [advisor's name] is an excellent speaker. We always get great feedback from the customers who attend his/her seminars. You're going to hear some important information that will help you towards your financial goals. [Advisor's name] also wanted me to reach out to you to see if you have any specific topics you'd like covered or questions you'd like answered during the workshop.

Thank you! I'll see you tomorrow night.

Whether you talk to a live body or have to leave a message, this process will help reduce the number of last-minute dropouts and give you a head start on understanding why the registrants have decided to attend. It will also provide the opportunity to connect with your audience quickly and build trust rapidly.

Supercharge Your Workshop-Marketing Efforts

As mentioned earlier, there are several ways in which you can market your workshop. These include direct mailings to a select group of bank clients, posters in the branch lobbies, a banner on the bank's website, staff referrals, client referrals, and personal invitations via phone. Let's evaluate each in a little more detail.

Direct Mail: Direct mail involves the sending of letters to bank customers. Unless you somehow narrow your list of invitees, direct mail can be expensive and terribly inefficient. To ease the burden, ask the bank's marketing department for a list segmented by customer age, deposits, financial relationships with the bank, and zip codes. That way, if, for example, you are going to provide a workshop on retirement planning, you could target your mailing to customers aged fifty-five to sixty-five, with at least $50,000 in deposits and at least three financial relationships to the bank (checking, savings, mortgage, credit card, etc.), and who live in zip codes that are within a twenty- to thirty-minute drive to the workshop location.

Use postcards for your mailing pieces instead of letters. Not only are letters more expensive to mail, but they need to be opened in order to see the information; with a postcard, the recipient can immediately view the offer. Once the mailing has gone out, have your assistant or the bank's call center do a follow-up phone campaign to increase your chances of solid attendance.

Posters in Branch Lobbies: You can ask your marketing department or product partner to create and hang posters that advertise the workshop, but if you use this method to market your seminar, know that the quality of attendees will be hit or miss. I have seen twenty-somethings show up at an estate-planning workshop when posters were used to advertise it. I appreciated their eagerness to plan ahead but felt that might be just a little too far. Now, if they had attended with an elderly parent, that would have been a different story.

Banner on Bank's Website: A website banner is somewhat like lobby posters with respect to the hit-or-miss nature of attendees. If you use this method, make sure the webmaster builds in the capability to click through to an online reservation system. As soon as reservations come in, you or your assistant should send a confirmation email stating that you are looking forward to meeting the registrants and sharing valuable information with them. The webmaster can build an automated confirmation into the reservation system so that you don't have to send each email yourself.

A spin-off of this technique can be used to provide onsite educational workshops to employees of one of the bank's good business clients. You can then use the business's intranet to advertise the workshop.

Staff Referrals: With a little bit of time and training, the bank staff can be helpful in marketing your workshop. Share with them the key points of the upcoming workshop and why a customer would want to attend. Also, make sure staff members know the process for making a reservation on a customer's behalf. A confirmation email should go out to the customer, just as it would if the customer had made the reservation via the bank's website.

Client Referrals: Existing clients are some of the best sources for workshop invitees. Since your clients probably associate with people who are a lot like them, your clients are likely to invite people who are in the same economic position. In addition, by the time your clients' friends show up at the workshop, they have heard what a fantastic financial professional you are. The workshop will then give you an opportunity, in a non-threatening way, to solidify that impression.

An easy and effective way to get friends of clients to your workshops is to conduct a client-only workshop and encourage your clients to bring a guest. You may even hear some of these guests say that their financial advisors don't proactively reach out to them with timely information. Bingo! You now have an opening to establish a new relationship.

Another technique is telling your clients, at portfolio reviews or at client-appreciation events, that you are now offering second financial opinions to the important contacts (friends, family, business associates) of your clients. Position it as a service you have recently added for only your best clients.

Then, give several of your introductory brochures to your clients so they can pass them along to friends. Include your seminar calendar and suggest that your clients invite a contact to one of your workshops as a way to meet you.

Personal Invitations: One of the most powerful methods for getting people to attend your workshops is to call invitees yourself. You make the first call and have your assistant follow up on any subsequent calls. In today's digital world of email, texting, voice mail, and social media, we have lost the art of the personal invitation. Even if you do end up having to leave a message on voice mail, it is the personal touch of calling that stands out and counts. This is most effective with clients and referrals from your best clients.

Regardless of the marketing method chosen, it should not only create buzz among the bank's customers but among the bank's staff and management too. The specific marketing channels you will use depend on the objectives you have set.

Summary

If you are new to your financial institution, workshops can be used to grow your business and increase your presence in the minds of customers and staff. If you are a seasoned veteran and have been at your financial institution for some time, workshops will be helpful in replicating your best clients and capturing additional assets from existing clients. While successful seminars take time, planning, and effort on your part, the potential results are well worth the investment.

➢ Action Plan

1. Complete the Seminar Payoff Formula.

2. Decide on your targeted audience, objective, topic, content, workshop type, sponsor (if you'll use one), workshop format, reservation system, venue, and date and time.

3. Choose your workshop-marketing methods.

CHAPTER 5

Deliver Dynamic Presentations: Executing Workshops

*"The audience only pays attention as long
as you know where you are going."*
—Philip Crosby

NOW THAT YOU HAVE "the cheeks in the seats," you have to engage your audience. Therefore, throughout this chapter, we will cover a series of ideas, techniques, and procedures on supercharging your workshop efforts.

It's Showtime!

It's the day of your workshop. You have a good group of people committed to attend, you're prepared to deliver a rousing presentation, the food is ordered, and the room is set up and ready.

To ensure that things go smoothly, arrive early. Rushing in at the last minute only raises your level of anxiety and makes you look disorganized to those who came in sooner than expected. Arriving early also allows you to check the room set-up and change it if it is not the way you want it. Additionally, arriving early gives you an opportunity to make sure the technology is working properly. Check to see if your projector is centered, arrange flip charts, make sure you have pens that work, etc. Then, take a little quiet time to get your game face on. In other words, relax and visualize a positive outcome.

As your guests begin to arrive, strategically place yourself where you can greet them. The end of the registration table is often a good location. That way, by the time the guests reach you, they already have a nametag and you can address them properly. This is a key part of the relationship-building process. Also, if you have a client who is bringing a friend, this process can aid you in getting introduced by your client. Take a moment and find out what brought your guests to the workshop. This helps to build a relationship of trust, one that will hopefully turn the guest into a client, and you can use the reasons you gather in your opening comments and during your presentation.

Now I know that there might be times when a large number of attendees arrive and it becomes difficult for you to spend time with any one person or couple. Do the best you can, and at the very least, make sure to introduce yourself. As there are lulls in the registration line, you can always go back and spend a minute with the guests you missed.

Once everyone is settled, it's time to begin. You may want to have someone from the financial institution introduce you, tell a little bit about why management has decided to provide an investment program, and indicate why you were selected as the advisor. Your introduction should also include your qualifications and any other pertinent information that would enhance your credibility with the audience. This part should be as well choreographed as the balance of your presentation.

The Eight Elements of Winning Workshops

Realize that the purpose of any workshop is to inform, disturb, and motivate. You should inform your audience but not make them experts on your chosen topic. If you tell them everything you know, why do they then need you?

Next, you want to disturb. Attendees need to realize they have a problem. Whether it's not having enough money saved for retirement, the possibility of outliving their retirement assets, or figuring out how to pay for health care costs in retirement, guests should leave your workshop a little uncomfortable.

Finally, you need to motivate. Motivate them to come and see you, for you have the solutions to the problems and issues you will so deftly discuss in the workshop.

To do all this, you must incorporate the eight elements of winning workshops. Master these for unbeatable results.

Element One: Have a Powerful Opening. As you begin the presentation, make sure you have a strong opening. Your first few lines should grab your audience's attention and create a buzz. This can be accomplished in a number of ways. You could drop a hint of what you are going to tell them or ask a question that gets them thinking. For example, suppose you want attendees at a retirement income planning workshop to imagine their vision for their senior years; you could ask, "When you think of retirement, what do you envision? Traveling more? Spending more time volunteering? The good news is, with proper planning, you get to decide."

Or start with a compelling story, one with a strong moral centered on your subject matter. If you can personalize your opening, it will add power to the balance of your talk.

Element Two: Touch a Nerve. We've already mentioned that you want to disturb and motivate your audience, but you also want to establish your own credibility. Building credibility begins with convincing the audience to be receptive to your ideas.

To create this environment of receptivity, use your personality to show the audience that you are genuine. When you are viewed as authentic, your audience's level of trust in you increases; people are more likely to give credence to others whom they like and respect. During the workshop, you want to project an impression that you are someone worth listening to, an authority on the subject.

Once you have established your credibility, you must disturb your audience so you can move them to your ultimate objective, action. The easiest way to raise the participants' level of discomfort is through stories. Stories help your audience visualize and project themselves into a particular situation, such as retirement. Help them to see that by working with you and incorporating your ideas, they can have the retirement they've happily anticipated.

Element Three: Focus on Three Key Messages. At some point in your opening, you will want to share with your audience what you are going to tell them. Keep this to three key points. There is something magical yet powerful about the number three. Think about the director yelling, "Lights, camera, action!" or the marriage verse from Ecclesiastes 4:12 that is recited at so many weddings: "A cord of three strands is not quickly broken." Even Shakespeare knew the power of writing in threes, as exemplified by "Friends, Romans, Countrymen, lend me your ears," a famous line from his play Julius Caesar. Pay attention and you will see threes everywhere.

Even the outline of your presentation should be divided into thirds. Dale Carnegie, one of our greatest public speakers, said it this way, "Tell the audience what you're going to say, say it; then tell them what you've said." I think this is powerful advice to follow.

Element Four: Keep the Audience Engaged. Involve your audience in your presentation. This will add to their level of engagement and assist you in leading them to the next step. A great way to keep your audience involved is by asking questions, but how can you create ones that are engaging? Here are some tips.

First, know your purpose for asking the question. Are you trying to stimulate conversation, create controversy or stir the pot, elicit an opinion or response, or determine the audience's level of understanding on the material covered up to that point?

Next, ask meaningful questions, that is, questions that are important to your audience. Also, ask questions that have more than one right answer. That takes the pressure off your participants and increases the likelihood that they will respond.

Finally, suffer the silence. If you really expect an answer, don't jump back to your presentation too quickly.

What types of questions should you ask? Open-ended questions, ones without a simple yes or no response, are best if you want to increase audience participation. Simple yes-or-no questions can be effective if you want to make a quick point, but use these sparingly.

Another useful type of query is the situational question, such as, "Has this ever happened to you?" Or, "Remember how you felt when…?"

How about asking the controversial or provocative question? This is a question that asks your audience to think more deeply. For example, "What if the markets never recover? How could this affect your retirement?" Or, "If your health changed overnight and you were unable to work, how would this affect your retirement?"

Using a rhetorical question can also cause the participants to ponder a subject. You're not looking for an answer. You just want them to consider a point.

Polls, too, will keep participants involved. "By a show of hands, how many of you think...?" This will also help you determine if your presentation is connecting with the audience, and if nearly everyone is in agreement on a point, you can get group dynamics working in your favor.

Element Five: Increase Participants' Attention Spans. The attention of your audience will ebb and flow during your presentation. Use the following techniques to recapture and retain it.

Cueing the audience or preparing them for what they should expect can increase attention. Research bears this out. As already mentioned, in your introduction, let participants know what you are going to tell them.

Including topics that have personal significance will also increase an individual's attention span. People will pay attention to matters of health, finances, their future, employment, etc. In other words, people pay attention if they feel the material affects them directly.

Another effective technique is to take a break in the presentation from time to time. I don't mean a bathroom or smoke break. What I am talking about is stopping every ten minutes and asking for feedback or a response to a question, or having the participants complete an exercise.

Changing the speed, tone, pitch, and volume of your voice will also capture attention. For example, you can punch up a really important idea by leaning forward slightly and lowering the volume of your voice. The audience will have to strain to hear you, so use a decrease in voice volume carefully, but doing so will make the point. Use the tone of your voice to express your emotions in the presentation. If you are happy, sound happy. If you are concerned, sound concerned.

In addition, props can maintain the audience's attention. I once saw a speaker compare the changes in the ways we listen to music to the changes in the ways we invest. The presenter showed the audience a vinyl record, an eight-track tape, a cassette tape, a CD, and finally an iPod. He then went on to explain that the evolution that has taken place in audio media is just like the evolution that has occurred with investment choices. We have gone from individual stocks and bonds to mutual funds, ETFs, asset allocation funds, and managed accounts. Technology has improved music-listening *and* investment experiences.

Another effective prop can be a flip chart. It gives you the opportunity to be flexible in your presentation by using an illustration to make a point or to answer a question.

Element Six: Use Partners Properly. Using partners in your presentations can be helpful or detrimental. Let me start by defining the term partner. Here I am talking about anyone with whom you would share the stage. This could include folks such as a product wholesaler, attorney, or possibly someone from your broker-dealer's back office. Partners can be helpful if they enhance the overall experience and your standing with the bank's customers.

They can hurt your presentation if you turn the workshop totally over to them. Time and time again, I have seen seminar participants crowd around a guest speaker after a presentation so they can ask him or her their questions. At that moment, who in the room has all the credibility? The guest speaker.

I'm not suggesting that you should never use guest speakers. I believe they can add value to the discussion and credibility to you since you are the one who arranged for them to co-present.

What I am suggesting is that you maintain control of the presentation. If you hand off the reins to the guest speaker, you have abdicated the opportunity to demonstrate your credibility and expertise.

At every workshop, you must be the one to open and close. You must also be the person who facilitates the question-and-answer sections of the workshop. And you deliver the majority of the presentation. Let me give you an example. You decide to deliver a workshop on where and when to use trusts in a financial plan. You decide to invite an attorney to co-present with you. That person should be someone with whom you have an existing relationship. You don't want the attorney, later on, referring your client to his buddy in the investment business. You deliver the portions of the seminar that cover how to use a trust to accomplish various objectives in a financial plan, and the attorney covers the technical aspects of trust design. In this example, the attorney enhances the workshop experience without taking it over.

Element Seven: Craft a Strong Close. Your close is just as important as your opening, and therefore, you should spend just as much time developing it.

The close can begin by taking a moment to summarize the most critical point with a story, maybe one from an unnamed client. Then restate the objectives, all the points of your presentation. Don't forget to tell the audience why each of these points is important.

Finally, start your call to action with an evaluation form (see figure 5) designed to get feedback on the value of the workshop. This form can also be used to capture referrals by having space at the bottom for attendees to fill in the names of others who would appreciate the value of your educational workshops.

Figure 5: Workshop Feedback Form

[Workshop Title]

Your feedback is important to us and helps us improve. Thank you for completing this form.

Your name: _____

Your email address: _____

Your phone number(s): _____

Your mailing address: _____

Would you like a complimentary, no-obligation consultation with [speaker's name]?
- ☐ Yes
- ☐ No

I felt the speaker was _____ on the workshop topic.
- ☐ very knowledgeable
- ☐ somewhat knowledgeable
- ☐ not at all knowledgeable

I felt the speaker was _____ for the presentation.
- ☐ extremely prepared
- ☐ somewhat prepared
- ☐ not at all prepared

I felt that this presentation was _____.
- ☐ extremely valuable
- ☐ somewhat valuable
- ☐ not at all valuable

What is your opinion of the location in which the workshop was held? Was it convenient? Was the temperature properly controlled? If the venue did not suit your needs, tell us what we should look for in another location.

_____

_____

Other comments: _____

_____

_____

If you felt this workshop was valuable, please provide the names and contact information for others who could benefit from being invited to our future workshops. Thank you.

_____

_____

_____

Notice that the top of the form contains a section asking the respondent if he/she would like a complimentary consultation. The participant can check *yes* or *no*. (The form should also include a place for the attendees to provide an email address so you can continue to stay in touch with participants via your client relationship-management system.)

Your call to action goes like this:

> *An evaluation form is in your workshop materials. We use this form as a way for you to give us feedback on how we did today. We are always looking for ways to improve our workshops and to make them more valuable for the customers of the bank, so please take a moment to fill out the form. My assistant will be at the back of the room to collect the evaluations as you leave.*
>
> *Also, you can use this form to let us know whether or not you would like to take advantage of a complimentary consultation. This is a no-cost, no-obligation, one-hour consultation that we offer to all who attend our workshops. If you check 'yes,' I promise that my assistant or I will be in touch with you in the next twenty-four hours to arrange a time when we can meet. In fact, if you have your appointment calendar with you, please feel free to schedule a time before you leave today. We have blocked out times over the next couple of weeks just for this purpose. And, if you do check 'no,' I promise that neither my staff nor I will contact you. Regardless of whether or not you have decided to take advantage of the consultation, I hope you found the information presented tonight both informative and worthwhile.*

Simple, effective, and I believe one of the most efficient ways to close a workshop.

Of course, make sure you collect the evaluation forms. If you don't have a strategy, many of the attendees will walk out with them. I have two suggestions. One is to position yourself at the back of the room near the door so that you can thank your guests for coming as you collect the evaluation forms.

Another effective method is to have a prize drawing from all the evaluation forms you collect. That gives attendees more of an incentive to complete the forms and turn them in. The drawing may be for a book on the subject you just covered or it could be for several novelty items. Your product partners can be a great resource for those items. It is interesting to watch how participants are engaged in this little contest.

Element Eight: Rehearse, Rehearse, and Rehearse Some More. Rehearsing your presentation is the critical element that will give you the confidence you will want to portray to your audience. If preparation time is limited, spend most of your rehearsal time on perfecting your opening and close. The body of the workshop shouldn't take much preparation time since this is material you work with every day.

Rehearsing will also help you to become a deliberate speaker, eliminating fillers such as *um* or *ahh*. You can minimize this tendency by rehearsing in front of someone else and asking him or her to keep track of the fillers used. Better yet, record yourself rehearsing; then listen to the recording so you can hear exactly where you use the fillers. Keep practicing and recording until you have eliminated them.

The Follow-Up

Once the room has emptied and everything is back in its place, your work is not yet done. Your post-workshop activities are critically important. Your next step is to call all the attendees who indicated they would like an appointment and who had not yet scheduled a time. Remember, you promised to get in touch within twenty-four hours, so start calling the next morning. The longer you wait, the colder these leads will become.

You, not your assistant, should make that first follow-up call so you can continue the wonderful relationship you have already established. This will also give you an opportunity to qualify the attendees by getting some additional information. If you don't reach some participants, leave a message and thank them for coming. Let them know you are looking forward to meeting with them and that your assistant will be in touch to schedule a time.

You may also want to think about confirming the ones who, after the workshop, did schedule an appointment with you. As you make these calls, begin by again thanking the attendees for coming to your workshop, and then let them know what documents and statements you would like them to bring to the meeting.

I also encourage you to call the no-shows if you had any. You never know what happened. They may have had every intention of attending but had an unexpected emergency that made them unable to make it to the workshop. Offer them an opportunity to come to your office, receive the handout materials, and review their financial situation with you.

Also consider sending out a press release on the workshop. Let the local business journal and newspaper know. In addition, ask the bank to put an article in their newsletter.

ABCs of Workshop Delivery

Here are some basics I want you to remember as you prepare to deliver your workshop.

Sell the Benefits. Focus on the benefits for your participants. They want to know what's in it for them. Be sure you tell them.

Be Different. Standing out from the crowd is important. You need to demonstrate during your presentation that you are different from the masses. You might be asking yourself: How do I do that? One way is to deliver a presentation that is educational *and* entertaining. First, you want to come across as knowledgeable, accomplished, and confident. Then entertain by sharing a humorous story that is pertinent to the workshop topic. Not a joke, mind you, but a story. Or, here's a really crazy one: learn to juggle. Then, at the beginning of your workshop, while you are juggling, talk about how difficult it is to juggle an investment portfolio while you are withdrawing money from the account. Go on to say, "If you're not careful…" and let the balls drop. I can almost guarantee that your audience members will not have seen that act before. Remember that you are not selling products at this presentation, you are selling yourself. When you are different, you are memorable.

Master the Silence. Mark Twain once said, "The right word may be effective, but no word was ever as effective as a rightly timed pause." Getting comfortable with the moments of quiet during your seminar and basking in the silence is a very powerful technique for capturing your audience's attention. On occasion, as you are presenting, suddenly stop talking and wait. Observe where all the attention is. On you. As mentioned earlier, this is an easy way to make an important point you would like your audience to remember.

Connect with Your Eyes. Establish rapport and connect with each workshop participant by making and holding eye contact for at least five seconds. If the person with whom you make eye contact looks away, appears bored, or seems uninterested, move on to a friendly face. This is one reason smaller, more intimate workshop groups work well.

Use Smiles and Facial Expressions. Smiling helps you convey a positive, warm vibe. So does nodding while participants are asking questions or making comments. Affirming their questions, thoughts, and ideas is a constructive activity when attempting to connect with all the participants.

Remember, Perception is Reality. Perception truly is reality in the minds of the attendees. Be sure your key messages are short and succinct.

Embody the Traits of a Great Speaker. All great speakers have certain personal traits: likeability, confidence, empathy, and depth of knowledge. You have to be likeable. It's pretty hard to trust someone you don't like. Use the pitch, volume, and rate of speech to demonstrate that you are confident in your ideas for helping people to, for example, retire successfully. Empathizing with your audience lets them know you are aware of their uneasiness with financial matters. Finally, the depth of knowledge you demonstrate during your workshop will give attendees the impetus to do business with you.

There is one last point I would like to make. A great workshop will kick-start your word-of-mouth marketing for the next seminar. If you deliver value-added, educational workshops to the bank's customers, your reputation will precede you and make it easier to pack the room with qualified attendees the next time.

Summary

You've made a significant investment in getting clients and bank customers to your workshop; now it's time to deliver an outstanding experience for your attendees. It's much like running a marathon. You've completed your training and managed your nutrition, and you're rested and ready to go. Now you're stepping up to the starting line. It's race day!

Begin with a powerful opening, leave your attendees with an impactful call to action, and cover material from your day-after-day appointments in the middle. And just like a runner who has a post-marathon recovery routine, make sure you quickly follow up with attendees after your workshop. Remember that time, especially the twenty-four hours that follow your workshop, is critical. You or your assistant must call every attendee the next day.

Now it's showtime! You're ready! Relax, have fun, and enjoy the run.

➢ Action Plan

1. Arrive early and check the layout of the room.

2. Test all equipment.

3. Take a quiet moment to get your game face on and prepare yourself mentally.

4. Greet your guests as they arrive.

5. Deliver a winning presentation!

6. Next day: call all the participants.

CHAPTER 6

Attract New Business Effortlessly: Gaining Referrals

"In sales, a referral is the key to the door of resistance."
—Bo Bennett

OPRAH WINFREY IS ONE OF THE BEST-KNOWN television personalities of our time. A mere mention or endorsement of your product or service by her could make you a millionaire. So what would be the impact on your business if Oprah were one of your referral sources? While you might not be able to count Oprah herself as part of your elite clientele, you do have several mini-Oprahs in your practice.

If you have an existing book of business or have inherited a book, this is one of the more important chapters for you.

In previous chapters, I have discussed the crisis of trust in today's society. As a financial advisor, it is critical that you break down the barriers that come from lack of trust. Developing your own Oprah Winfreys is one strategy that will do this.

The importance of client referrals has been drummed into us by our managers from the first day we called ourselves financial advisors, and if you have ever had a client or influential individual introduce you to someone else, you've experienced the clout and cachet that comes with a personal referral.

Referral Sources

Let's start by listing all the referral sources available to you:

- ➤ Financial institution staff
- ➤ Financial institution management
- ➤ Centers of Influence
- ➤ Strategic alliances
- ➤ Clients

The management and staff at the financial institution are interacting with multiple customers on a daily basis. You want to make sure your co-workers are equipped to recognize opportunities for your services and have the script for making the referral and *connecting* you to those customers. We will talk more about this in the next chapter. Branch managers, in particular, will have knowledge of the more influential customers. You should position yourself as a partner who can help them with those customers' total financial needs.

Malcolm Gladwell, author of *The Tipping Point,* introduces the concept of *connectors* by recounting the midnight ride of Paul Revere. While there is much historical debate about what happened that evening, there are lessons to be learned. According to Gladwell, Paul Revere was very active in the politics of the day and was respected and known by many. This familiarity and respect made him credible. Therefore, when he sped along on his horse and called for the militias to spread throughout Lexington, they came. As you look for individuals you can develop into centers of influence or with whom to build strategic alliances, you'll want to focus on finding connectors like Revere.

Finally, you will want to focus on developing your clients as referral sources. Getting referrals from your clients is a purposeful way to build your business, particularly if you focus on your best clients. It is a solid method for replicating the top of your book year after year.

If that is the case, and we know it is, then why have financial advisors been so unwilling to ask for referrals? A huge part of this reluctance is due to the financial advisor's fear of hearing *no* from the client, fear of endangering the client relationship, or fear of looking needy.

Let's focus on a strategy that makes it easy for you to ask for referrals and for your clients to give them. There are three steps.

1. Make yourself referable.

2. Build a client advocacy program.

3. Create the trust-based referral process.

Make Yourself Referable

Do a quick check to assess how referable you are today. Start by answering the following questions: Are you getting all the referrals you deserve? Are you getting unsolicited referrals? Do the referrals you get fit your definition of quality referrals? Where are your referrals coming from: Staff? Management? Centers of influence? Strategic alliances? Clients? Do you have fifteen to twenty consistent referral sources?

How'd you do? If not very well, here are several actions you can take to increase your referability:

➤ Write down your description of your ideal client.
➤ Articulate, exactly, the benefits of working with you. What value does a person gain when he or she becomes your client?

➤ When you receive a referral, follow up immediately.

➤ Thank the referrer once you have received a referral.

➤ Ensure your work is of the highest quality every time. Commit to improving your processes daily.

➤ Be likeable! This is essential.

➤ Become a referral source for others. Remember, as you give, so shall you receive. Furthermore, when you give a referral, make it an awesome one.

It is also important to have the proper attitude when you design a client referral strategy. It's an easy three-step process.

1. Admit that if you are not getting referrals, it's your problem, and if you're not getting quality referrals, it's your fault.

2. Commit to improving your referral practices. That starts with asking for what you want. If you want referrals, you need to ask for them. Every time you have contact with a client, particularly with your best or ideal clients, you need to remind them that you accept referrals.

3. Stay in touch and spend time with those who consistently give you referrals. In order to be seen and stay top of mind, you need to be visible. Spending time with your referral sources helps deepen the relationship, which, over time, improves your likeability.

Build a Client Advocacy Program

The purpose of a client advocacy program is to get word-of-mouth marketing working for you by having your best clients sing your praises and spread the good news about what you can do for their family, friends, and co-workers.

Here are some principles of advocacy I want you to understand and embrace.

- > Become an advocate for your clients first. That means in all your dealings with them, you do what is best for the clients, not what is best for you.
- > Understand that advocacy is a function of friendship and loyalty. Know your best clients at a deeper level. Spend quality time with them outside of the office. It's part of being likeable.
- > Make sure you are adding tangible value to the relationship.
- > Know that what you do for them is what really counts. For example, you help them prepare to pay for health care costs in retirement, generate a steady retirement paycheck, organize their important documents such as health care powers of attorney and living wills, and review beneficiary designations.

This strategy creates clients who are more loyal, and loyal clients are profitable clients. Russ Alan Prince of Prince and Associates, a leading market research firm in the realm of global private wealth, has talked about the financial rewards of having loyal clients. His research has shown that an average client will bring you $17,000 of additional assets over the life of the relationship whereas a loyal client will bring you an additional $376,000. Focus on the connectors, those individuals who are well known and respected. Typically, these are people who also enjoy helping others by making introductions. It takes ten average clients to get one referral while a single loyal client gives an average of 11.8 referrals over the course of the relationship, so it definitely pays to have more loyal clients.

Here is a six-step program to getting them.

1. Ask your clients for their expectations of you as their financial advisor. You can do this as you conduct their quarterly reviews.

2. Tell your clients what to expect. What level of service are you going to give them? How much access will they have to you? What are the benefits of having you as their financial advisor?

3. Create ways for your clients to provide feedback. The easiest way is through any of the available online feedback or survey tools.

4. Carefully listen to what your clients say, and act on what they tell you.

5. Implement suggested changes and then let your clients know what changes were made as a result of their feedback.

6. Repeat!

In addition, utilize the following strategies.

Create a Client Advisory Board. Developing a client advisory board is another way to generate really loyal clients. This involves asking some of your best clients to sit on a committee modeled along the lines of a board of directors, a board that will help you become the best advisor possible. By asking for their feedback, you are creating a group of individuals that now has a vested interest in your business. People like to be asked for their opinion and are willing to help if you make the request.

Pick the clients who embody the qualities you would like in your board members. Think about their availability, willingness to help, and influence (are they connectors?). Then, at a portfolio review meeting or via a phone call, tell these clients that you respect their opinion and ask them to participate. This isn't something you do through a letter.

Once you form the group, meet on a quarterly basis. The agenda items might include a review of your branding and/ or marketing materials, a discussion of your sales and service processes, or your client communication program.

Executing the client advisory board strategy will help you refine your processes into something clients want and appreciate. An additional benefit will be a steady flow of high-quality referrals from your board members, and you won't even have to ask because they are engaged in your business and have a feeling of ownership in its success.

Segment Your Book. To execute the whole client advocacy program strategy really well, you will need to segment your book into A, B, C, and D clients if you haven't already done so. Top clients are As; less desirable clients are Ds. If you have a large book, this could be a very involved task. If that is the case, then at least segment out your A clients, as well as the B clients who have the potential to become As.

When segmenting, consider factors beyond assets that clients have invested with you. Think about revenue (if you have a large managed-account business), whether or not you enjoy working with the client, whether or not the client accepts your advice, or other features that appeal to you. You may want to think about building a points matrix, one in which you assign a certain number of points to each client's characteristics, to guide you as you work through your book. It might look like table 4.

Table 4: Client Points Matrix

Assets Under Management	Points Assigned
$1,000,000 and above	5
$500,000 to $999,999	4
$250,000 to $499,999	3
$100,000 to $249,999	2
Below $100,000	1
Intangibles	**Points Assigned**
Client gives me referrals	Yes = 3, No = 0
Client is a connector	Yes = 2, No = 0
Client has high potential for future business	Yes = 2, No = 0
Client has other business with me (e.g., life insurance)	Yes = 1 No = 0
I enjoy working with this client	Yes = 1 No = 0

You would then, based on the total points assigned, categorize or segment the client as an A, B, C, or D. This is not an exact science. You still need to use your judgment. The segmentation or categorization matrix might look like table 5.

Table 5: Client Segmentation Matrix

Client Tiers	Total Points
A Clients	10+
B Clients	7–9
C Clients	4–6
D Clients	1–3

Once the segmentation process is complete, create an extra-mile client service table. This involves determining the level and types of services you will provide to each client tier. For example, perhaps clients on the A tier will get a quarterly review of their investment or retirement plan while D clients will only get an annual review letter from you. Your A clients and their friends will receive invitations to client-appreciation events while the rest won't. Your A clients will have your cell phone number and the rest will not. The point is that your best clients will get the most attention, service, and value from the relationship. Your activity matrix might look something like table 6.

Table 6: Tier Activity Matrix

Activity	Tier A	Tier B	Tier C	Tier D
Phone Call or Newsletter	Monthly	Quarterly	Annually	As Needed
Portfolio Reviews	Quarterly	Annually	Annually	Letter
Financial Plan	Yes	No	No	No
Client-Appreciation Events	Yes	No	No	No
Client-Education Events	Yes	Yes	No	No
Webinar Invitations	Yes	Yes	Yes	No
Birthday/Holiday Cards	Yes	Yes	Yes	No
Has My Cell Number	Yes	No	No	No

As you build your activity matrix, you need to give thought to your support structure and how you will deliver the promised service levels. Here are a few tips:

- ➤ Automate your client service processes using your available technology to its fullest.
- ➤ Develop a repeatable process for client reviews.
- ➤ Review the job functions of all your support staff and assign all non-essential activities to them.

Make sure you engage your staff in the discussion so that you have their support and they understand the importance your business is placing on providing world-class client service.

Once your matrix is built, you want to actively communicate these service levels to your best clients. The objective is to let them know they are special.

The Trust-Based Referral Process

Once you begin to implement your overall client advocacy program and your extra-mile client service activities (table 6), how do you overcome your fear of asking for referrals? I recommend using the trust-based referral process.

This starts with the dialog you have with your best clients during each interaction, the dialog during which you say that you are offering free portfolio reviews to referrals. This will accomplish two things. First, you will have an opportunity to meet others who probably behave like and have the same financial needs as your best clients. Second, you will be introduced to your prospects by someone they know, which is likely their preferred method for meeting a financial advisor.

Now you are positioning referrals from a level of strength. You are demonstrating a desire to assist and in the process, reminding your clients why they have chosen you as their advisor.

The next step in the trust-based referral process involves giving your client a press kit. A press kit is information about you, your staff, and your business. Some call it a capabilities kit or an introductory kit. It can be a spiral-bound series of pages, a three-ring binder, or inserts in a pocket folder that your client can give to interested friends, family, and co-workers.

The press kit includes a personal bio written to introduce you as an individual and *doesn't* use the typical corporate bio format of where you went to school and where you have worked. It also doesn't include the standard corporate headshot but should include a photo of you in a more natural pose. The bio should talk about you as a person and emphasize the values that influence your investment and planning philosophies. Potential clients want to know you warmly; they want to know who you are as an individual first before they will trust you with their money. Here is an example of one advisor's personal bio:

> *Let me tell you a little bit about myself and my investment process. Since January of 2001, I have been providing wealth management services for the customers of Your Hometown National Bank and their families.*
>
> *My wife and I are avid golfers. There are similarities in developing a plan for playing each round of golf and developing a plan for retirement. In golf, each hole presents new challenges and obstacles: distance, wind, bunkers, water hazards. After each stroke, some obstacles are eliminated and new ones emerge. You have to be prepared to change your game plan, and so it is with your retirement plan. As we develop your investment and retirement plan, we will meet on a predetermined schedule in order to make adjustments that will keep you in the middle of your financial fairway.*

Other elements of the press kit include:
- Team bios and roles
- A review of the process you use for determining the potential client's financial goals
- The investment process you use
- A list of the products and services you offer

The client can give the press kit to acquaintances who ask, "Who are you using for financial advice?" This way, the client can introduce you and the prospective client can meet you in a non-threatening manner.

The final step in your strategy for gaining excellence in referrals is to execute on the plans you have put in place. Make this a part of the overall strategic plan you worked on earlier.

Summary

Yes, an endorsement from Oprah can generate a lot of business for a particular product or service, but you can use a similar principle to your advantage as well. Just develop the mini-Oprahs you have in your clientele. Designing and utilizing the processes described in this chapter will help you meet others who are just like your best clients.

➤ Action Plan

1. List the names of all your potential referral sources, including staff, clients, centers of influence, and strategic alliances.

2. Measure your referability.

3. Build your client advocacy program.
    a. Create a client advisory board.
    b. Segment you existing clients.
    c. Develop your client service matrix.

4. Create a trust-based referral process utilizing a press/introductory kit.

CHAPTER 7

Establish a Winning Team: Staff Training

"Giving people self-confidence is by far the most important thing that I can do. Because then they will act."
—Jack Welch

HAVE YOU EVER BEEN AGGRAVATED while sitting still on a four-lane highway? Of course you have. There isn't a metropolitan area in the country that doesn't suffer from a rush hour traffic jam. When you are attempting to get somewhere on a timely basis, a halt in the flow of traffic can be frustrating. Similarly, when it comes to the flow of potential new clients to your financial services business, keeping all inbound routes open and full of referrals is important, and the branch referral route is just as vital as the routes from clients, centers of influence, and strategic alliances.

To get the staff at your institution's branches to make referrals to you, you have to help the employees understand what you do, why you do it, why you are part of the institution's product offerings, and how to make referrals. Branch referral training is the way to do this, and it can be helpful to you in driving new business, particularly if you are new to the financial institution and just building your clientele. Branch referral training can happen just about anywhere—from the breakroom to a branch meeting—and anytime you are in contact with the staff.

Features of Branch Referral Training

Just like your clients, bank employees would like to know you as a person…as a spouse, parent, hobbyist, member of the community, etc. They also want to know about your qualifications for helping customers with their non-banking financial needs. For example, are you a CERTIFIED FINANCIAL PLANNER™ professional or working towards becoming one?

Help employees see that you are partnering with the financial institution to offer financial products over and above the traditional products provided by banks and credit unions. You need to help the staff comprehend that like the other bank employees, you are there to help customers with their financial goals. Help the personnel to see you as one of them and not as an outsider siphoning off bank assets in order to collect commissions, and not as someone sitting in the bank on your way to a better job opportunity. Let them see you as somebody who is committed to the financial well-being of the customers.

It is also important for them to see what you do and how you do it. Give them an idea of the problems your clients face, such as paying for health care expenses in retirement; converting an investment portfolio from the accumulation phase to the income phase in the face of inflation, volatile markets, low interest rates, and longevity; or trying to retire without an employer-provided pension income.

Share the challenges of the sandwich generation, those trying to care for elderly parents while sending their children to college. Help the staff perceive the value you bring to clients when you get them to appreciate the need for a will, trust, or health care power of attorney and then put them in touch with a lawyer who can prepare the necessary legal documents. Don't forget to cover the problems you solve when you help a client determine the need for life or long-term care insurance.

How to Conduct Branch Referral Training

Demonstrate what you do by providing your services to the staff and delivering a workshop on a specific financial topic, just like you do for your clients. (See chapters 4 and 5.) Become known as the expert who helps employees allocate their 401k contributions. While you can't give specific advice on which funds they should invest in, you can provide general asset allocation recommendations based on employees' retirement timelines.

It's important that the staff members recognize how you partner with the bank to further provide financial security to bank customers. This might take place through a single-need approach or a more comprehensive one depending on the requirements and desires of the customer. Spend some time talking about the supervisory process the bank conducts and how your recommendations are reviewed to make sure you are doing the right thing for your clients each and every time.

Be specific; show the staff actual cases where you helped someone solve a financial problem through a recommended planning technique or product solution. Be as clear as you can without divulging confidentialities, identities, or a customer's circumstances. Spend time documenting the types of problems your ideal clients face so you can give the staff a road map to the type of customer they should be referring to you.

The Training Calendar and Agendas: Take time to plan out your branch referral training calendar and training agendas, and pay careful attention to the interactive parts or your training sessions. Make sure the participants are having fun so they stay engaged. Prize drawings are a good way to do this. The items don't have to be expensive. Trinkets from your product partners will do nicely. You could also give prizes for the most correct answers on a quiz.

As you create your training agenda, think about the objectives you have for the participants. You want them to:

> Find you trustworthy enough to make referrals to you
> Identify qualified prospects
> Make the transition to a referral

Tell them that when you get a referral, you will follow up immediately and do what is in the customer's best interests. Act as if the staff has had a bad experience with a previous financial advisor and you are trying to win them over. That's a great position from which to frame the discussion.

As you build your training program, think about whom you should be training. The list includes:

> Personal bankers
> Tellers
> Loan officers
> Personnel in call centers
> Branch managers
> Senior management

Each of these groups may require a different setting for the training. For example, you might provide training to the tellers in the lobby fifteen minutes before the branch opens, while the senior management might receive your training at a staff meeting in the boardroom. Some financial institutions have training days on bank holidays, like Presidents' Day. If that is the case, make sure the training director blocks out time for you on the agenda.

Of course a critical question is: *When should you conduct training?* I suggest taking advantage of every opportunity you get. Since the staff may be targeting and getting evaluated on achieving goals in several programs—for example, mortgage referrals, new account openings, credit cards, as well as your financial advising program—it's hard for employees to keep you top of mind. Therefore, you will not want to miss any chance to train. Opportunities that will present themselves include:

> ➤ One-on-one sessions
>   – Breakroom conversations
>   – Slow times in the teller line
> ➤ Branch and department meetings
> ➤ New-employee orientations
> ➤ Employee training days

Who should provide the training? Initially it should be you. Remember, the staff wants to get to know you. After you provide the initial training, your assistant and product partners can deliver subsequent sessions. Product partners generally have programs that are specifically designed for this purpose.

In addition, you can call on your branch advocates to conduct training. Branch advocates (see Branch Advocacy Program in chapter 3) are individuals you've identified in each branch who champion your program when you are not there. You want to select personnel who, in the past, have been good supporters, as evidenced by the number and quality of referrals they've sent you. When branch advocates conduct training, they remind other branch employees of your program, show them how to refer customers, and enhance your credibility in the eyes of the branch staff since the personnel being trained see that one of their colleagues is already referring customers to you.

The Referral Process: When conducting training, show the employees how to identify a customer's financial needs and then, once identified, how to make the referral. Give them the actual words they should use. In fact, role playing can be an effective way to demonstrate the technique. Motivate the training participants by giving a prize for the best role play.

You may also ask individuals who have given you referrals in the past to share their experience: How did they come upon the customer? What triggered the identification of a need for your services? How did the employee make the referral?

Incentives for Staff Referrals

Many financial institutions give a financial incentive to staff members when they provide a referral to the institution's investment advisor. If your bank or credit union doesn't have this sort of incentive program, talk to your compliance department about implementing one. These programs differ from institution to institution. Some may only provide a five- or ten-dollar incentive for every qualified lead, but *qualified lead* might mean nothing more than someone who keeps an appointment with the financial advisor.

On a monthly or weekly basis, report the referral results by individual and by branch to get a little friendly rivalry going. You may want to purchase a top prize that is rotated among the staff on an annual basis; make it a bit of a competition.

Anytime you have the opportunity to thank someone publicly you should, so also use the monthly or weekly reports to express your appreciation. Furthermore, reserve space in the report for those who provided referrals to share how they identified the referral opportunity, what they said to the customer, and how they eventually made the referral.

Finally, have a conversation with the leaders of the financial institution, suggesting they add an incentive piece to the compensation of the branch managers. Branch managers who reach or exceed their referral goals should receive additional remuneration in their paychecks as part of their total compensation package. These incentives will create additional branch-level advocates for you and your program.

Summary

Because financial institutions have many products that the staff is responsible for selling or personnel to which the staff must provide referrals, it is difficult for you to stay foremost in employees' minds. Therefore, you need to continually remind the staff that you are there to help customers with their long-term financial goals.

As you provide branch referral training, remember that the staff wants to know you as a person *and* they want to know that they can trust you with a referral, so train every chance you get. Don't even let a five-minute opportunity slip by.

➤ Action Plan

1. Build a branch referral training calendar.
   a. Work with the individual at the bank who is responsible for managing the branches.
   b. Arrange dates, times, and locations.

2. Build a branch referral training agenda. Make it comprehensive and then adjust according to the time you have available.

CHAPTER 8

Grow Your Relationships: Planning and Conducting Client Events

"Great hearts steadily send forth the secret forces that incessantly draw great events."
—Ralph Waldo Emerson

AUSTIN, THE CITY IN WHICH I LIVE, offers a vast number of events for its residents and visitors on any given day. A bout between two teams from the Texas Rollergirls, a league of female roller derby competitors, is one of the more unusual events I've attended. Just like Austin, you should be offering a number of events to your clients...not necessarily every day, but at least a few times a year. Client events should be an important part of your business development activities. They are a way to build stronger relationships with your best clients outside of your normal business meetings and should become a large part of your client advocacy program (see chapter 6).

Taking time to plan your events properly will be well worth the effort. How do you know if you've hosted a great event? Just pay attention to the reactions of your clients over the following days, weeks, and even months. If, on their subsequent visits to your office, they are still thanking you for inviting them to the event, then you know it was a great one. If you have other clients asking how they can get invited to the next one, that's another signal that you hosted a great event.

Event Objective

The purpose of any event is to deepen your relationships with your best clients, retain existing business, capture assets currently held at other financial institutions, and obtain referrals to prospects whose profiles match those of your best clients.

While all events are meant as a way for you to say thanks for the confidence your clients have placed in you over the past year, you will need to decide whether you want a gathering to be a recreational event or an educational one. Your agenda will drive the location and activities for the event, but whether your plan is for fun or for edification, you must build in time for socializing.

Over the last few years, smaller more intimate events have dominated because they make it easier for you to emotionally connect with the attendees, thus deepening the overall relationship. Small events give you the opportunity to have a one-to-one conversation with all who are present.

Matching Your Invitation List to the Event

Deciding whom to invite to the event depends on the agenda. If you want to have some fun with your best clients on the golf course, then invite clients who enjoy golf. How do you know if they enjoy golf? Ask them.

As you get to know your clients better, tidbits about their likes and dislikes will naturally come out in conversations, but until then, you could survey your clients to find out what they're fond of doing in their spare time. I like the survey approach because you can design the questionnaire to gain insight about clients' leisure activities and other information as well. You can use any online survey system, many of which are free.

As you profile your clients, you may uncover several different groups such as:

- ➤ Golfers
- ➤ Gardeners
- ➤ Sports fans
- ➤ Foodies
- ➤ History buffs
- ➤ Artists
- ➤ And many more

Track this information in your client relationship management system, and then plan your events around groups with a common interest. For the foodies, schedule a private class at a cooking store. Stores usually charge for classes, but you can negotiate a free after-hours cooking class by purchasing gifts for your clients at the store. In addition, remind the store owner of the additional revenue he or she will reap when your wealthiest clients shop in the store after class.

For clients who are history buffs, arrange a scavenger hunt at a local museum. You could then have drinks and snacks catered in after the hunt.

To offset any costs, arrange financial support from one or two of your product partners. Your event is an opportunity for the partners to add value to your business and get their products' names in front of your clients.

If you schedule an educational event, you can bring in an outside speaker, but as with workshops (see chapter 4), make sure the guest speaker does not upstage you. Again, your product partners can be helpful here. Depending on your level of production, one of them might be able to supply an economist or portfolio manager from his or her firm.

CPAs and attorneys are also excellent choices as guest speakers. Just ask a CPA to talk about tax planning and your clients will respond in droves. Or partner with an attorney who specializes in estate planning or elder care to host a valuable event for your clients.

To maximize attendance at an event, send a confirmatory letter to your clients after they have indicated they'll attend and include four tickets with that letter: one for your client, one for his/her spouse or significant other, and two for guests that the client would like to invite and who might have an interest in the topic. In the letter, ask the clients to call the office if they'll be bringing guests. That way, you will have all the visitors' information, and nametags will be ready for them when they arrive.

Your Roles at the Event

Regardless of the type event, make sure you act as the greeter. Making a connection with the clients and their guests as they arrive is important in setting the tone of your event. Consider having a welcome table that is manned by one of your staff. There, the attendees will pick up their nametags and any materials, sporting equipment, utensils, etc. that they will need prior to the beginning of the event.

Position yourself at the end of the table so you can say hello to the attendees as they pass and introduce yourself to anyone you do not already know.

Your next role is that of the master of ceremonies. You open the event, introduce the educational topic or explain how the recreational outing will play out, and if you have guest speakers, you will introduce them. As master of ceremonies, you will also wrap up the event by thanking everyone for coming and close with, what I call, the painless referral method. This involves thanking your clients for their business and the trust they have placed in you.

Continue by thanking them for the individuals they have referred to your office and how you have been able to help many of them with their financial issues. Finally, offer a free portfolio review to your clients' friends, family, and colleagues. Does this sound familiar? It should; it is analogous to the trust-based referral method we discussed in chapter 6.

If any of your attending clients have given you a referral in the past, then they'll react with an internal *you're welcome.* If they have not given you a referral, this technique is an easy and painless way for you to let them know that you do in fact accept referrals.

Post-Event Follow-Up

You must follow up with your clients and guests *the next day.* Mail personalized, individual letters thanking each attendee for coming and participating. If you hosted an intimate or smaller client event, send a handwritten note. Handwritten notes are rare these days, so receiving one will reinforce the great impression you hopefully made during the event. While you are writing your follow-up thank-you notes, your staff should be calling each client who attended to schedule an appointment that addresses any issues that arose during the event, such as moving assets, changing beneficiary designations, or purchasing long-term care insurance. In addition, have your team call guests of clients to thank them for coming and to arrange for an initial meeting with you.

While you might think the next-day follow-up is a no-brainer, you would not believe the number of times that I have witnessed its omission. If an advisor doesn't follow up with the attendees or waits too long before doing so, the effect of the event is minimized and opportunities are lost.

Follow up internally, too, by tracking your results. You will want to track the number of attendees, the number of follow-up appointments scheduled, the additional assets you captured, and the GDC (gross dealer concession) or revenue generated. Track the expenses too so you can calculate the exact return on investment of each event.

Summary

Client events can be a great way to build your business and solidify relationships with your best clients. To make every client event a great event, profile your clients so that you have an understanding of their personal likes. This will allow you to plan specialized events around them.

Be the greeter and master of ceremonies. You need to be seen as the director, the one in control. Don't hand off this important image-building activity to someone else.

Follow up with all attendees the next day.

Finally, track your results. Know the financial investment for each event and record the financial results each event yields in the form of additional revenue and assets under management. Soon you will see the impact client-event marketing has on your business and your income.

➤ **Action Plan**

1. Select a group of clients with like hobbies, interests, etc.

2. Plan an appropriate event for this group.

3. Conduct the event.

4. Follow up with the attendees.

5. Track the results.

CHAPTER 9

Master High-Gain Sales Techniques: The Selling Process

"I never failed once. It just happened to be a 2000-step process."
—Thomas Edison

WHEN MEETING WITH PROSPECTS, you must establish trust, nurture an ongoing long-term relationship, and cultivate the potential client's confidence in you. You won't be able to get to the high-gain sales process if you can't adequately accomplish these objectives first. A well-designed process that you use time and time again will help you keep track of what you still need to do to close a sale, especially if you have multiple cases open at once.

Tracking Processes: Lessons from Thomas Edison:

Thomas Edison's ideas didn't always work right away, but he did not see himself as a failure. Such was the case in his development of a practical incandescent light bulb.

Over an eighteen-month period, the inventor tried thousands of different ideas until he came up with the one that worked. When asked about his tenacity, he replied, "I have not failed.

I've just found 10,000 ways that won't work." He established a process for tracking the various tests he conducted so he wouldn't lose time repeating experiments that didn't pan out.

You must do the same. To help your clients achieve their long-term financial goals, you must also establish a process, one that is carried out orderly and efficiently by following one step at a time. The more efficient your process, the more customers you can help, and in the end, the more clients you will have.

If advisors do not repetitively follow a proven process, they will skip or forget certain steps along the way. When you omit steps, you lose sales. Financial advisors who understand this are disciplined in charting the progress of each new prospect. The most disciplined keep an electronic spreadsheet of all their activity.

The Business Model

There are basically three business models on which to build your sales process: product specialist, investment generalist, and wealth manager.

Product Specialist: The product specialist focuses on a single product such as annuities, managed accounts, or mutual funds. This is the model towards which most advisors gravitate because it is easy and focuses on plucking the available low-hanging fruit.

Investment Generalist: The investment generalist provides a range of products to solve clients' financial problems. The investment generalist usually gathers a minimal amount of information, just enough to determine product choices and an asset-allocation strategy.

Wealth Manager: The wealth manager uses a comprehensive method for helping clients manage their financial lives. These advisors focus on knowing the nature of all assets and understanding the goals and desires of their clients. This is the smallest group of advisors, and adopting the wealth-management model might be a way to differentiate your business.

While you can make a good living following any of these models, I am partial to wealth management for several reasons. First and foremost, people, especially baby boomers, need the help of wealth managers. Folks born between 1946 and 1965 have been good consumers, but they have not been very good savers. In addition, the majority will retire without a defined-benefit pension plan and didn't do a good job of setting money aside in their 401(k)s or similar retirement accounts. Since they will live longer than their parents, baby boomers will also need to deal with the cost of their health issues in retirement.

The assistance they need doesn't end with the plan you prepare for them. Future economic conditions will require vigilant attention in the years ahead, right up until their death when any money remaining is distributed to their heirs. If you do a respectable job of meeting and developing relationships with the heirs, you stand a greater chance of retaining the assets.

When you adopt a wealth-management model, it is easier to sustain high-gain sales because you're building a strong brand and a solid reputation for your business. These are qualities that will last regardless of economic cycles or regulatory environments.

In contrast, while the product specialist and the investment generalist can make a good living, they typically do not fare as well as the wealth manager year in and year out. Products fall out of favor due to market or regulatory conditions, which in turn, cause production revenue to ebb and flow. In addition, product specialists and investment generalists have not deepened their client relationships; consequently, they do not uncover opportunities to help their clients in multiple ways.

Furthermore, at the death of their clients, they lose the assets to the heirs' financial advisors.

The Sales Process for Your Business Model

Your broker-dealer may suggest a sales process to you. If so, review the steps to see if they will work in your business model.

However, I favor a process developed by my colleague and friend Jack Crawford, a sales manager who has coached and mentored many top bank-channel advisors over the years. Here are his steps:

1. **Ask, "How can I help you?"** This simple question is the trigger for starting the sales process and gets right to the heart of what brought the prospect into your office. Once you ask this question, let the person identify his or her issue.

2. **Transition to front talk.** Your front talk is where you review who you are, your processes, and any compliance information you may need to supply such as the fact that the investment products you sell are not insured by the bank.

3. **Describe your planning process.** Walk prospects through your sales process so they understand what will happen if they select you as their investment advisor. Also mention your points of differentiation. Why should the prospect do business with you and your bank and not the advisor across the street? Then get permission to move to the next step by asking, "How would you like to proceed?"

4. **Gather information.** If the prospect indicates that he or she would like to move forward with you, use

a form that will aid you in getting all the prospect's information. Over time, you will get very proficient in asking the questions in a natural, conversational tone.

5. **Sum up the information you have recorded.** Give prospects your personal assessment of the information they have provided. Let them know what they've been doing well and what you believe still needs to be addressed. Verify that the prospects agree with your assessment.

6. **Begin to identify recommendations.** Once you have agreement from the prospect that you have accurately captured and assessed the information, give a couple of preliminary recommendations. You are looking for an initial reaction. If the reaction is negative, probe deeper into the goals and objectives. You may have missed or misunderstood a critical piece of information.

7. **Say, "Great! Then here's what we'll do."** Begin laying out the next steps. Address items that can be handled immediately. If you are using a multistep process, then lay out the items you will cover in your next visit. If there are items to be handled in the future, such as a retirement plan rollover, then cover those as well.

8. **Outline the communication and review process.** Mention how often you communicate with your clients, what methods you use, and the procedure for conducting a portfolio review.

This eight-step process assures that you have taken a holistic approach, provided value, given direction, and gotten the agreement to proceed.

Similarly, you will need to develop the following elements to generate your high-gain sales process:

- ➤ High-gain trust-building
- ➤ High-gain questioning and listening
- ➤ High-gain technical planning
- ➤ High-gain framing and storytelling

We will focus on the first two in this chapter and the latter two in the following chapter.

High-Gain Trust-Building

Nineteenth-century German philosopher Friedrich Nietzsche once wrote, *"I'm not upset that you lied to me, I'm upset that from now on I can't believe you."* His words are as meaningful today as when he first wrote them. We all know the importance of trust in a selling relationship, so the question then becomes: How do we earn the trust of our prospects? Are there specific actions we can take that will lead to a trusting relationship as quickly as possible? Before we answer those questions, do the exercise in figure 6. It will get your juices flowing for the rest of this chapter.

Figure 6: The Advantages of Building Trusting Relationships

What benefits would surface if your prospects and clients trusted you more?

- _____
- _____
- _____
- _____
- _____

In *The Speed of Trust*, author Stephen Covey states, "Trust is a function of two things: character and competence." He goes on to say, "Character includes your integrity, your motive, your intent with people. Competence includes your capabilities, your skills, your results, your track record. Both are vital."

Business specialists David Maister, Charles Green, and Robert Galford, authors of *The Trusted Advisor*, state that:

1. Trust grows rather than appears.

2. Trust is both rational and emotional.

3. Trust presumes a two-way relationship.

4. Trust is intrinsically about perceived risk.

5. Trust is different for the client than it is for the advisor.

6. Trust is personal.

They provide the following formula for building trust:

$$\text{Trust} = \frac{\text{Credibility} + \text{Reliability} + \text{Intimacy}}{\text{Self-Orientation}}$$

Let's look at each piece of the formula in more depth so we can answer the questions posed earlier: How do we earn the trust of our prospects? Are there specific actions we can take that will lead to a trusting relationship as quickly as possible?

Much goes into **credibility**. It deals with the words you use to explain planning ideas and products to your clients. It has to do with your professional development; for example, are you a CFP®? Prospects and clients will even judge your credibility by how engaged you are with them in the interview. Are you in the moment or do you appear distant?

Reliability is all about doing what you say you will do. If you tell a prospect that you will have an investment plan completed in a week, and two weeks later you still haven't called, then your reliability will be questioned. If you tell a client that you will handle a withdrawal from her investment account and a week later she still doesn't have the check, your reliability will be shot. You get the picture.

Intimacy is a tough one. Maister, Green, and Galford state that lack of intimacy is one of the more common reasons for failing to build trust. What does intimacy mean in a business setting and how can you get to that place? When clients honestly share their biggest dreams and their deepest financial fears with you, you have reached a high level of intimacy. Clients have become comfortable enough and safe enough with you to share that information. The fastest way to reach that level of intimacy is to share information about yourself. The authors warn, however, not to share too much too quickly, for it can backfire. Let your instincts be your guide.

Having low **self-orientation**, which is a positive attribute, means you are more concerned about helping clients achieve their financial goals than you are about making the sale. Having annual reviews with your clients to make sure they are staying on track towards their financial goals even when there is no chance for a new sale is a good sign of low self-orientation. It's putting your clients' interests ahead of yours.

Now you should be able to see how the formula operates. By increasing the values of the components of the numerator (credibility, reliability, intimacy) and decreasing the value of the denominator (self-orientation), you will increase the level of trust in the relationship. Let's work through an example in figure 7.

Figure 7: Whom Can You Trust?

Step 1: Write down the name of someone you trust.

Step 2: Now think about:

- Why you trust this person

  _____

  _____

  _____

- How the relationship started

  _____

  _____

  _____

- The point in the relationship at which you knew you could trust this person. Was it an event or did it progress over time?

  _____

  _____

  _____

Step 3: Now rate this person on each element of the trust equation.

Credibility (C)   1 2 3 4 5

Reliability (R)   1 2 3 4 5

Intimacy (I)   1 2 3 4 5

Self-Orientation (S)   1 2 3 4 5

Step 4: Calculate trust: T = (C) ____ + (R) ____ + (I) ____ / (S) ____

Now that you see how the formula works, do the following:

1. Make a list of the behaviors that you believe are key to developing trust.

2. Make a list of behaviors that can quickly destroy trust.

Review your business actions to ensure they are congruent with developing trust quickly and early in your high-gain sales process. Put yourself in your customers' shoes and decide if you would trust you. How many of the trust-building behaviors that you listed are incorporated in your business? For your maximum benefit, give this serious consideration.

Trust is essential to success in our professional and personal lives. Trust is important to the satisfaction and joy we experience. You are selling a relationship, one that will develop and grow over the years. When you can cultivate a long-term relationship with a new-found client, you will be rewarded with additional assets and referrals.

High-Gain Questioning

Regardless of your business model, your questioning process should demonstrate your desire to truly assist clients with their financial future. The importance of questioning skills is often overlooked by advisors.

Asking questions goes beyond the just-the-facts-ma'am approach of *Dragnet*'s Sergeant Joe Friday. *New York Times* journalist Mary Rowland, in her book *Best Practices for Financial Advisors*, states, "The relationship between a person and his money is complex, mysterious—and often secret. Psychologists call money the last frontier in therapy."

Certainly you have been in situations with clients who've had an attachment to a specific company's stock, shared financial information with you that they didn't want their spouse to know about, or wanted to only invest in a fixed annuity because of the perceived safety even though their financial goals would not be realized through this choice. Your questioning skills need to be precise and fine-tuned in order to get past all the emotions surrounding a client's nest egg.

How do you ask good questions? What is the best process? Start by asking factual questions since they are easier to answer. Then move to the harder and more emotional questions.

Here are three tips for successfully asking questions.

1. **Ask more open-ended questions than close-ended ones.** You know you need to ask some close-ended questions such as, "What is the value of your 401k account?" but you also need to ask questions like "When you imagine yourself in retirement, what are you doing?"

2. **Use silence to your advantage.** Silence is a tool that allows you to get at more difficult emotional information. Because your client will likely find silence to be uncomfortable, he will naturally continue talking to fill the gap. That's when you might get the most valuable nuggets of information.

3. **Ask clarifying follow-up questions.** By asking clarifying questions, you will be letting your potential client know that you are not only interested in the answer but in completely understanding it.

Many companies will provide their advisors with certain data-gathering tools such as worksheets, questionnaires, and surveys. While these materials can be helpful in gathering basic information, they generally don't go deep enough and they normally don't touch emotions. You will need to develop your own set of questions to supplement the factual information you are gathering.

I'm sure you have an arsenal of preferred questions you've refined over the years and use in your current sales process. Use table 7 to write down some favorite questions you like to ask potential clients. Then think about why you asked those questions. What were you attempting to uncover? Also think about whether you have been getting the depth of information needed. Finish by designing follow-up questions based on potential answers and results.

Table 7: What Are Your Favorite Questions to Ask?

Initial Question	Reason for Asking	Follow-up Questions

Refreshing your questions or adding new questions can bring a new energy to your information-gathering process.

High-Gain Listening

Listening skills sit at the apex of the high-gain sales process. How well you listen to the answers from the powerful questions you ask will have an important impact on your effectiveness as an advisor. You can't design the right plan without carefully considering the responses given during the fact-finding interview. Listening will also impact the quality of the relationships you will develop with individuals if they should become clients.

Unfortunately, our minds are often working on other issues while we should be actively listening to our clients. How, then, do you become a better listener? It starts with being interested in your client. Having genuine interest in your prospect or client will keep you zeroed in during the meeting. Next, you must be fully present by minimizing distractions. Turn off your computer screen, mute your computer speakers, silence your cell phone, and get out from behind your desk.

At the start of each day or at the end each previous one, prepare a to-do list so you're not trying to make a list in your head when you should be focused on your prospect or client.

Hearing what is being said is only the first the part of the listening process. You also need to *understand* what is being said, and then you need to *evaluate* what you heard. Understanding comes from encouraging people to finish their thoughts and by asking clarifying follow-up questions. For example, you could say, "That's interesting, please tell me more," or "If I understood you correctly you said… Is that right?"

Once you understand what has been shared, you need to use your experience and professional judgment to evaluate the responses. Caution: don't let bias cloud your judgment. Keep an open mind.

Why You Need Good Listening Skills

Good listening skills will help you be more productive. Having strong listening skills will allow you to:

> ➣ Better understand your clients' needs and desires in relation to their stated financial goals.
> ➣ Increase the trust your clients have in you. We talked about this earlier; good listening skills help create intimacy.
> ➣ Resolve problems quickly and efficiently.
> ➣ Provide the right answer to a client's question the first time.

➤ Find the underlying meaning in what your clients are saying to you.

High-gain questioning and listening skills will enable you to quickly build trust with your current and potential clients. Failure to execute these skills properly can be a way to rapidly erode the trust you have built. Strong questioning and listening skills will allow you to better serve your clients, and in the long run, isn't that why we are in the financial services business?

Summary

Trust building, the first skill in the high-gain sales process, can be learned and takes time.

Strong questioning and listening are the second set of skills in the high-gain sales process. These skills will assist you in getting the answers needed to build the proper financial, retirement, or investment plans for your prospects and clients. Listening goes beyond hearing the words that were said; it also involves discerning the intent.

In the next chapter, we will cover the final two elements of the high-gain sales process: high-gain technical planning and high-gain framing and storytelling.

➤ **Action Plan**

1. Complete the exercise: The Advantages of Building Trusting Relationships.

2. Complete the exercise: Whom Can We Trust?

3. Complete the exercise on reasons for trusting and not trusting someone.

4. Complete the exercise: What Are Your Favorite Questions to Ask?

Get to the Close:
Handling Objections

"It takes as much energy to wish as it does to plan."
—Eleanor Roosevelt

ONCE YOU HAVE BUILT TRUST, gone through the discovery interview, and used your new questioning and listening skills to capture all of your client's important information, it's time to use your technical skills to create a solution and then present it. In other words, now it's time to combine the first two skills of the high-gain sales process with the next two skills, high-gain technical planning and high-gain storytelling and framing.

High-Gain Technical Planning

You will need to be a lifelong learner in order to always be capable of preparing technical plans that will enable your clients to achieve their financial goals. So how do you become one? Read, read, and read some more. The financial services industry is filled with available sources such as technical journals, how-to manuals, and industry publications. Additionally, reputable websites offer a great deal of information on every financial topic.

Other sources include industry organizations' workshops and meetings. These sessions give you access to the industry's best ideas, techniques, and practices. The time and money spent joining and attending professional association meetings will be well worth it for the new approaches, investment solutions, and practice management skills you'll gain.

Table 8 lists a few of the resources you might consider putting in your lifelong-learning toolkit.

Table 8: Resources for Lifelong Learning in the Financial Services Industry

Journals	
InvestmentNews™	Research Magazine
Bank Insurance & Securities Marketing	Bank Investment Consultant
Investment Advisor	Boomer Market Advisor
Financial Advisor	Journal of Financial Service Professionals
Journal of Financial Planning	
e-Newsletters	
401k Advisor Bank Investment Consultant	
Trade Organizations	
Financial Planning Association Society of Financial Service Professionals American Society of Pension Professionals & Actuaries	

The best advisors stay on top of their game by constantly developing their knowledge base. Their quest for up-to-date information allows them to remain technically competent in an ever-changing financial landscape and prepare the best financial plans for their clients. Others decide to pursue additional designations too.

Software programs have made it easy to prepare a by-the-numbers financial plan, but don't forget to incorporate your experience and intuition when designing a financial solution for a client. While there are several really good software programs available, each has its limitations. Your broker-dealer may offer you some as part of his or her value add-on. Review those and see if any make sense for your business.

High-Gain Framing and Storytelling

At this stage of the sales process, you have built trust, asked great questions, listened intently to the answers, and used your technical competence to put together the perfect financial solution for your client. Now it is time to deliver that solution in a manner that allows your client to understand why this is the best way to achieve his financial goals and dreams. That is where framing and storytelling become important.

Framing means selecting and explaining one solution that will solve your client's problem instead of presenting multiple solutions. The latter approach confuses the client and leads to frustration and lost sales.

To properly frame the discussion around your core recommendation, consider the client's key requirements and/or financial goals *and* how the proposal addresses them. For example, you might frame the discussion by saying, "You've worked hard all your life; now it's time to enjoy a worry-free retirement."

Use an agenda (see sample in figure 8) to help in the framing process.

Figure 8: Sample Client Presentation Agenda

ABC Bank Investment and Retirement Services

Meeting Agenda

Date: August 10, 2012

Type of Meeting: Review of Financial Plan for a Worry-Free Retirement

Client: Mr. and Mrs. Bank Client

   I. Discuss any new issues since previous meeting.

  II. Review gathered financial information.

  III. What does a worry-free retirement mean to you?

  IV. Verify financial goals.
     A. Review income needs for a worry-free retirement.
     B. Review legacy objectives.

  V. Deliver recommendations from financial plan.

  VI. Finalize implementation plan.
     A. Determine action steps.
     B. Assign responsibility for follow-up activities.

  VII. Set date and time for next meeting.

You will also want to have a blank copy of your implementation plan template. As you are reviewing your recommendations, you will want to get confirmation of the next steps; write them down and immediately assign responsibility. A sample, with some steps filled in, can be found in table 9.

Table 9: Sample Implementation Plan

ABC Bank Investment and Retirement Services			
Implementation Plan for Mr. and Mrs. Bank Client			
August 10, 2012			
Action Step	**Who is Responsible?**	**Due Date**	**Progress**
Determine current beneficiary designations on all accounts	Mr. Client	September 1, 2012	Assigned
Run long-term care illustrations for Mr. and Mrs. Client	Advisor	September 1, 2012	Assigned
Complete and sign annuitization paperwork	Advisor	August 10, 2012	Assigned
Develop legacy planning for grandchildren	Advisor	September 1, 2012	Assigned

Storytelling is a form of communication that is as old as human language, and it's still around because it works. Purposeful stories reach prospects and clients amazingly quickly. Such anecdotes help people get the message without the slow and painful accumulation of evidence and reason. Consider which is more powerful: a technical discussion of how standard deviation works as a measure of a portfolio's volatility or a good story about risk and reward.

Here is an example of a story you could use with a client who enjoys golf.

> *When you're watching the final round of a golf tournament on television, you often hear the commentators refer to the 'Sunday pin placement.' As you know, that means the flag is placed in such a way as to tempt the professional with a risk-versus-reward dilemma. If the golfer goes for the pin, he might be rewarded handsomely with the championship trophy and a big payday, but if he doesn't hit that perfect shot, he could end up in big trouble, potentially falling several places back on the leader board. On the other hand, the golfer could play it safe by going for the center of the green. He may end up in second place, but he will still go home with a nice paycheck. Investing is the much the same.*

A good story captures the mind, imagination, and interest of the prospect or client.

Why Storytelling Works: If you presented the same information to two separate groups with one group offered the information as a list of facts and the other offered the information in the form of a story, the second group would retain more of the information. Why? Because of the way our brains are wired.

Using a Morningstar report to demonstrate the alpha, beta, and ten-year performance history of a particular mutual fund or discussing how diversification in a portfolio reduces the overall risk is important, but it is also very left-brain oriented. According to Scott West and Mitch Anthony, authors of *Storyselling for Financial Advisors*, left-brain activities represent only 10–20 percent of the successful sale. The other 80–90 percent come from the right-brain functions.

The left side of the brain analyzes information and agonizes over the decision, but it is not where decisions are made. The right side puts all the information together, understands how the proposal will benefit the customer, and makes the decision. Storytelling touches the right side. This is where people visualize how your proposal can help them achieve their financial goals and dreams. By engaging the whole brain in your presentations, you will maximize the impact of your solutions and shorten the overall sales process.

Learning to speak the language of the right brain will improve your ability to articulate, clarify, and win over your clients. To help you develop the language, pick some of the topics below and then build a story to go along with each.

- Importance of Diversification
- Investing for Growth vs. Value
- Stocks vs. Bonds
- Significance of Investing Internationally
- How an Annuity's Living Benefits Work
- The Value of Annuitization for Retirement Income
- Using Insurance for Wealth Transfer
- Other

Now commit these stories to memory so you can draw on them when needed.

Handling Objections

I have often thought that the close to a sale is a bit like the exchange between a parent and child at the checkout line of the grocery store when the child spots an impulse item retailers so cleverly place at the child's eye level. The child grabs the item, holds it up to the parent, and exclaims; "Get this for me!" The parent says "No," and from there the debate is on, the parent calmly explaining why the child may not have the item and the child expressing how her life will not be the same without the toy or candy. The child persists in the hope of wearing the parent down.

We have all witnessed this scene and some of you may have even been a party to it. I have also witnessed this exchange between adults. The financial advisor recommends an investment and the prospect pushes back, doubting the investment is for her. It is not a method I would recommend in sales.

To be successful, you will need a strategy for handling objections effectively and professionally.

An objection can take on several forms. It may be nothing more than a question or a need for additional information, or it could be a genuine concern or a downright stall. Handling objections requires a professional, non-defensive approach. No salesperson likes to hear an objection, but it goes with the territory. In fact, if the prospect isn't asking clarifying questions, you probably don't have a buyer. A lack of questions indicates a lack of engagement in the process.

One way to answer objections is to anticipate them. Consider the potential objections or questions that might be raised about the products and services you sell. Then analyze those objections and come up with clear, factual, and concise answers to counter the doubts. Focusing on your high-gain questioning and listening skills will help you accomplish this task. In fact, if you address potential objections and questions in your presentation, you may be able to prevent the prospect from voicing them.

A Six-Step Approach to Handling Objections: If objections, questions, or concerns do arise, here is a six-step process to help you handle them.

Step One: Listen. Don't be quick to respond. Use silence to your advantage. It creates an uneasy tension so that in time, the client will share with you the entire reason for her concern. Once you feel like you have heard the entire objection, let silence fall between you before you answer.

Step Two: Feed the objection back to the prospect. Restate what you heard. This will ensure you understand the concern, indicate you are listening, and give the client or prospect an opportunity to clarify and to provide additional information if necessary. By being certain that the client has expressed the entire concern before you answer, you will minimize the chance that the concern will arise again. Also, once you have all the information, your eventual answer to the objection will be more complete.

Step Three: Spend time examining the objection. As the client asks the question or states the objection, avoid the tendency to begin formulating your answer in your mind because the first objection you hear may not be the real one. Give the customer time to completely express himself, and then ask follow-up questions to clarify the concern. This step will enable you to have the full and real story behind the apprehension.

Step Four: Answer the objection. After you're confident that you have the whole story, address the concern with conviction and confidence. If appropriate, use materials such as reports or charts to support your response.

Step Five: Validate your answer. Check that your answer was not only heard but understood. Confirm that the prospect or client is comfortable with the response you gave. Accomplish this step by asking, "Does that adequately answer your question?" Failure to complete this step increases the likelihood that the question or objection will be raised again

Step Six: Move on. Once the objection, question, or concern has been answered, get back to the remainder of the recommendations. Start your next sentence with "By the way..." to get back on track. For example say, "By the way, did I mention that the investment growth is tax deferred?" Remember those three words, for they will serve you well in redirecting the conversation.

The more you use this process, the more effective and efficient you will become. But what happens if you begin to hear objection after objection? If that happens, you need to redirect the conversation back to the original goals your prospect or client expressed in the discovery interview.

The Close

Now that you've gathered all the information, prepared your case, and adeptly delivered your recommendations using high-gain framing and storytelling, it's now time for the big close, right? Wrong!

The idea of a big close is outdated. Your close should be something as simple as "To get your plan started, we just need to fill out some paperwork. Is that OK?" Nothing more. If it becomes more than that, you probably missed a critical step along the way. You may not have completely understood the client's financial objectives. You may not have built enough trust or rapport. If you were unsuccessful in closing the sale, reexamine the steps you took to see if a missed step becomes clear.

Summary

Building technical expertise and staying current on the most recent developments in the industry take time and commitment. Realize that being a lifelong learner of the business is not only advantageous to your client but advantageous to your general health as well.

Properly framing your presentations and delivering them with stories increase the likelihood that the information will be understood, believed, and acted upon. Speak the customer's language and stay away from industry jargon.

Now it's your turn to put the high-gain sales process together with the skills you have already developed over your career. Build the right foundation and then refine your techniques appointment after appointment.

However, *understanding* the high-gain sales process is much easier than *executing* it. It takes commitment and discipline to fit these activities in every day but doing so will pay dividends for you and your future clients.

Find a repeatable process that works for you and then stick to it. Over time, you will become so proficient and confident that your overall sales will increase.

➤ Action Plan

1. Prepare a self-development plan.

   a. Subscribe to the journals and newsletters (electronic or hard copy) that you will read each month.

   b. Research relevant professional organizations and then join the ones that are the best fit for you.

   c. Decide which professional designations you will pursue.

2. Create templates for meeting agendas and implementation plans.

3. Complete the build-a-story exercise.

4. Review and practice the steps for handling objections.

CHAPTER 11

Work Smarter Not Harder: Managing Your Business

*"After one look at this planet any visitor from outer
space would say 'I want to see the manager.'"*
—William S. Burroughs

IMAGINE FOR A MOMENT that an alien from an orderly,
well-managed solar system landed here on Earth and took a
look around. The first thing that alien might say is, "Who is in
charge here? We need to talk!"

Without proper management, whether on a planet or in a
business, pandemonium ensues. As the manager of your financial practice, your role is keeping your business organized and
on track as you work to achieve your own goals and deliver the
client experience you've promised. To do this, you will need to
closely monitor three sets of processes: client contact, resource
management, and sales and event activity. If you simplify and
systematize these processes, they will happen daily without
your direct input. Let's look at each of these in more detail.

Client Contact

Client contact involves updating clients' information, resolving problems, responding to clients' questions about their accounts, keeping them informed about relevant topics and issues such as the current market conditions, conducting account reviews, and developing a client advocacy program. (For this last element, see chapter 6.)

Because the financial services business has become so commoditized, advisors can no longer differentiate themselves based on the newest product, better returns, or the slickest new financial planning software. We are in a relationship business; that means we can differentiate ourselves via client and prospect communication. It's amazing to me that so few companies are seemingly unable to treat customers well and respond to them in a timely and professional manner. To me, that's basic. It should be a given, but quite often, it's not.

Here are some tips to incorporate into your client contact processes.

Provide timely answers. Clients want their concerns to be answered quickly, but they also want them answered correctly. If an issue cannot be resolved immediately, commit to calling the client back at a specific time with an answer or update.

Be courteous and respectful. Clients call because they have an issue, a service request, or a question they couldn't answer on their own. Now put yourself in your clients' shoes and think about a time you've called a customer service line to get a situation resolved. If the experience was pleasant, the attitude of the individual on the other end probably had much to do with your feelings after the call. On the other hand, if you got a good helping of a bad attitude, your opinion was probably totally different, even if the issue was resolved in your favor. Make sure your staff is aware of this important client-first mindset.

Have a process for handling inbound calls. Help all staff members understand what calls they should handle and what calls need to be elevated to you. Write down the criteria. That way, if you have staff turnover, training a new employee becomes much easier.

Make sure your staff is knowledgeable. Having well-trained staff is important to a smoothly operating office and reinforces the confidence your clients have in you. I'm not suggesting that your staff be credentialed in financial services, but they should know the difference between an annuity and a mutual fund, between bonds and equities, and between nonqualified and qualified investments. Spend some time making sure your staff understands these basic financial concepts.

Be a good listener. Making sure you understand a client's question or issue can save everyone time and energy. It also demonstrates to your clients that they are important to your business. For details on developing your listening skills, see chapter 9.

Follow up. Once the issue has been resolved, get back in touch with the client. This little step can be a great way to differentiate your business and build goodwill.

Resource Management

You have several resources to assist you with the growth of your business. These include time, talented people, and money. As you build your business, you need to track the use of your time, engage others in your vision—whether they work directly for you or not, and identify the financial sources that will facilitate your cash flow. Let's examine each of these.

Time: Is it just me, or do you feel like there is less time to accomplish all your daily assignments? One of the major differences between average performers and top performers is that top performers use their time wisely.

Stephen R. Covey dedicated his life's work to assisting people in becoming more effective and productive in their personal and professional lives. In his book, *The 7 Habits of Highly Effective People*, Dr. Covey states that to effectively manage our time, we must *organize and execute around priorities.*

He developed a method of sorting tasks into four quadrants (categories) based on the importance and urgency of each task. To help you take advantage of Covey's method, use table 10 to list and describe all the tasks you need to complete. Just do a brain dump; don't worry about prioritizing just yet.

Table 10: Task List and Descriptions

Task Title	Description of Task

Now, transfer all those tasks to the appropriate quadrants in figure 9, which is based on Covey's practices.

Figure 9: Prioritizing Tasks

Quadrant 1 Important and Urgent 1. 2. 3. 4. 5.	**Quadrant 2** Important but Not Urgent 1. 2. 3. 4. 5.
Quadrant 3 Not Important but Urgent 1. 2. 3. 4. 5.	**Quadrant 4** Not Important and Not Urgent 1. 2. 3. 4. 5.

As you move forward in your business, you should have fewer and fewer items in quadrant 1. Covey refers to those who are always in quadrant 1 as people who are in crisis mode. If these people are not careful, activities in quadrant 1 keep getting bigger and bigger and lead to stress and burnout. If the item is important, you need to eliminate the urgency around it. Build a business process around the activity.

Let me give you an example. Adding new names to your sales pipeline is one of the most important tasks in your business. If this is not a constant pursuit, production and income take a roller coaster ride along a path of good and bad months. You fill the top of the pipeline and push the prospects through the sales process. As the results begin to spill out the bottom, you realize you need to reload. At this point, panic sets in and you frantically schedule a round of workshops and referral training sessions for the staff. Since it takes time for cases to run their course, you go from a strong month to a dry month as you deal with a new set of prospects.

Wouldn't your health, sanity, and paycheck improve if you had a steady flow of names traveling through the sales pipeline? You can get that and eliminate the urgency of this task by building a calendar that includes dates for workshops, staff training sessions, and activities in your client advocacy program.

Most of your time should be spent on tasks in quadrant 2, those that are important but not urgent. In fact, Covey said that these are the tasks on which you should focus to achieve your long-term goals. Delegate or eliminate the tasks that are in quadrant 3 (not important but urgent) and in quadrant 4 (not important and not urgent).

Review the way you completed figure 9 so you can decide which tasks you need to focus on, which can be delegated and to whom, and which activities should be eliminated or ignored.

People: In order to gain more time to work on specific activities that require your direct involvement, it's important to engage others in your business vision. An ancient Chinese proverb says, "Tell me and I will forget. Show me and I may remember. Involve me and I will understand." High-performing financial advisors know that it takes a team to generate large volumes of business year after year and to manage the business going forward.

People you can count as resources may include individuals who work directly with you, such as an office or sales assistant, and individuals who work indirectly with you, such as a branch manager or internal company associate.

You can monitor the activities of those who work directly with you by starting each day with a stand-up, fifteen-minute meeting. Everyone outlines their important actions for the day, and that gives you an opportunity to adjust as needed.

Money: Financial resources are available to you from your financial institution, the product wholesalers with whom you partner, and your personal financial investment in your business. To maximize the return on every dollar you spend on your marketing and client-building programs and achieve higher production, avoid a hit-or-miss reactionary approach and focus on an overall plan. The best way to accomplish this objective is through the annual budget process. Let me give you an example of how this would work.

Start by breaking your marketing budget into quarters. Then list the activities for each quarter that will require an investment. This might include a marketing campaign and a workshop and/or client-appreciation event. Each activity will have a price tag. Estimate the cost of each, add them together, and you have your quarterly budget. Add the four quarters together to get your annual marketing budget.

Once you know the amount required, look for available resources. Start with your bank or credit union. Have they allotted you a sales and marketing budget for your program? If there are multiple advisors in your program, talk with your manager to determine the amount available for your efforts. Assign those dollars first.

For the balance, you will need outside resources, so look to product partners next. Schedule individual planning meetings with the wholesalers with whom you work. Share with them your budget for the year and ask how much they would be able to contribute. Know this is a quid pro quo proposition so they will be looking for an estimate of anticipated sales into their lines of business. Don't worry about appearing presumptive in your expectation of receiving financial help from your wholesalers. They will appreciate your well-thought-out and planned approach and the fact that you consider them true business partners.

Resource Management Exercise: Use table 11 to assist you in thinking through the human and financial resources available to you in your business and how to best maximize their value. A few examples have been provided to get you started.

Table 11: Resource Management Worksheet

Resource	Type (Person, Financial, or Both)	How to Use Resource to Maximize Value
Branch Manager	Person	Form partnership for maximizing the branch relationships
Annuity Wholesaler	1. Person 2. Financial	1. Ask resource to assist with delivering workshop on retirement planning 2. Ask resource to sponsor one client lunch per quarter
Mutual Fund Wholesaler	1. Person 2. Financial	1. Ask resource to assist with market updates to clients 2. Ask resource to sponsor one client breakfast meeting per quarter
Sales Assistant	Person	Position resource as your client service specialist

Sales and Event Activity

The attainment of your goals requires tracking of your sales activity and your event activity, including workshops. The latter is critical for a steady flow of new and follow-up appointments with qualified prospects.

Activity management involves monitoring your position and weekly achievements in relation to your stated objectives. It is also about making sure you have enough appointments every week to attain your goals and about continuously filling the prospect pipeline.

Here is a list of the sales and event activity you need to track.

Sales Activity

- Appointments
  - With new prospects
  - Follow-up meetings
  - Reviews with existing clients

- Sources and Number of Activities that Generate New Prospects
  - Workshops
  - Referrals
  - Direct mail campaigns
  - Other marketing efforts

- New Business
  - Potential
  - Pending
  - Closed cases
  - Paid compensation

Event Activity

- ➤ Workshops (Refer to chapters 4 and 5.)
  - – Invites
  - – Attendees
  - – Appointments
  - – Business closed

- ➤ Referral training for the financial institution's staff (see chapter 7)
- ➤ Professional development/continuing education

Develop processes for capturing the above information into the appropriate weekly reports. See if your employer or broker-dealer provides a system for tracking this information. If not, develop your own spreadsheet. Then examine the reports to track your progress towards your weekly, monthly, and annual objectives.

Summary

To truly fulfill the promise of a high-performance financial services business, you must focus on managing client contact, resources, and sales and event activities. Some advisors make the mechanics of running successful financial services businesses complicated, and that's unfortunate. Running a successful business that will outperform the competition is straightforward. The key lies in execution.

High-performance advisors are skilled at using the most effective business processes of other successful advisors, putting those processes in place, and executing on them. The journey is worthwhile. Make the commitment to running a great business.

➤ Action Plan

1. List all your important tasks and prioritize them using the quadrant matrix.

2. List your available resources and determine how you will maximize their value.

CHAPTER 12

Achieve Peak Performance:
Balancing Your Life

*"Happiness is not a matter of intensity but of
balance and order and rhythm and harmony."*
—Thomas Merton

CLIENT DEMANDS, production deadlines, emails, phone calls, and increased access to all kinds of information through the Internet, combined with the ever greater pressures of family commitments and social activities, don't necessarily tip the scales in favor of living a balanced life.

Reaching balance is important but extremely difficult to accomplish. The challenge comes from the many roles we play: financial professional, spouse, parent, volunteer, athlete, etc. When you focus too much on one area, the others suffer from neglect.

I have witnessed so many colleagues who have achieved success in their professional lives but have had their personal lives shattered. So, what does it mean to live a balanced life? Does it involve complete nirvana where your soul and nature are in absolute harmony? Or does it encompass a life that is experiential and full in all areas? I believe a balanced life lies somewhere in between. It doesn't involve living a life completely devoid of stress because that would be boring. It *does* involve living a life that is in sync with your values.

Essentially, six areas of your life compete for your time and attention at any moment:

> ➤ Career
> ➤ Family
> ➤ Leisure
> ➤ Community Involvement
> ➤ Spirituality
> ➤ Health

Our devotion to each of these areas will ebb and flow based on demands, issues, and problems. Having balance in your life means that you are giving appropriate consideration to each area to minimize a constant give-and-take feeling.

Let's examine each of these facets individually, but keep in mind that they are all interconnected.

Career

Most of us will spend the majority of our waking hours on the job. It is a source of meaning, connection, and mutual support. Additionally, it pays the bills and fuels our lifestyles.

Not only do our careers provide financial rewards, they also deliver emotional benefits and feelings of accomplishment. As we progress in our careers, they can also provide us with greater self-esteem and a sense of who we are. After all, we will even introduce ourselves by referencing what we do for a living: "I'm a financial planner" or "I'm a retirement income specialist." It becomes a piece of our identity, but if we end up living and breathing our careers, then we are bound to experience an unhealthy level of stress and a life out of balance.

Family

When we are young, our families influence our personalities, help us develop our social skills, and contribute to our understanding of love, self-confidence, honesty, and generosity, characteristics that are important to living a successful life.

While you don't choose your relatives and they don't choose you, they still provide a cocoon of safety and support, assisting you as you navigate the ups and downs of building a financial services business. Your family members can furnish a heavy dose of encouragement as you face the challenges in your career, and they will celebrate with you as you hit important milestones.

Just as your family influenced you, the environment in your home influences your children. Therefore, spend time with your spouse and children, not only in one-on-one situations but as a complete unit. This time is special, so leave your cell phone or PDA in the car. Doing so will help you to stay focused and in the moment.

Living a balanced life also includes keeping in touch with extended family members and those who do not live near us. While our busy lives make this more difficult, cell phones, websites like Facebook, and applications like Skype and Facetime have made it much easier to stay engaged.

Leisure

When did you last do the things you really enjoy? With endless obligations, we often have very little time for leisure activities, but they help us relieve stress and distract us from the pressures of life. Recreation gives us a sense of self, brings about a positive flow of energy, and refreshes the mind.

You can choose any activity that suits your tastes. Learn to dance, play an instrument, hike, camp, fish, swim, try an adventure sport, or do something less strenuous like watching a movie with friends and family or reading. At the end of the day, all that matters is a feeling of rejuvenation.

Community Involvement

Volunteering can help fulfill a deep human need to benefit others. Any organization will appreciate whatever time you can donate, even if it's just an hour a month.

Be aware of the difference between volunteering as a way to fulfill the need to give back to society and volunteering as a way to market your business. However, marketing your business can be a natural result of being actively engaged in the community.

You can find a host of groups that can benefit from your assistance: youth teams that need coaches, organizations that help those with an infirmity, and many more. The list of non-profit organizations is extensive, and so many agencies need a pair of helping hands. Think of something you enjoy or are passionate about, and then find an organization that addresses that passion or issue.

Volunteering may also be a way for you to double-dip in your quest for a more balanced life. As you are exploring organizations and charitable activities with which to become involved, look for opportunities where you can participate with your family. Kids find out that there are all sorts of people in the world when they get involved in community outreach, and this discovery can serve them well as they mature into adulthood.

Now is the time to put your experience and skills to good use, meet new people, and make a difference in the lives of others.

Spirituality

As humans, we are naturally spiritual beings. Spirituality means different things to different people. For some, it is expressed as a religious experience, while for others, it refers to insight and understanding. Regardless, engaging in spiritual activities—whether attending a house of worship, taking a meditation class, or spending more time in natural settings—helps you realize when something is missing in your life. It creates the desire for you to get back in balance, so embrace a belief system that makes life pleasant for you.

Health*

If you are going to work hard, you need to have the energy and health to enjoy the fruits of your labor. Diet allows us to maintain an optimum body weight and provides the fuel for our daily activities. Exercise, while also helping with weight control, gives us the energy and stamina to live the balanced life we desire. A healthy lifestyle also increases self-esteem and confidence, which are important elements for success in the financial services business. I am not interested in turning you into an Athena or Adonis or even into the next marathon champion of your community, but I am interested in sharing some tips on how to have the energy, stamina, and health to enjoy all of the areas of your life we have already discussed. It is hard to enjoy that balanced life when you're too tired or too sick to enjoy the journey.

---

* Health recommendations are for informational purposes only and are not intended to be a substitute for professional medical advice, diagnosis, or treatment. Always seek the advice of your physician or other qualified health provider with any questions you may have regarding a medical condition. Never disregard professional medical advice or delay seeking it because of something you have read in this book.

Exercise. The benefits of a regular exercise program aren't only for a marathoner or triathlete. Even if you never enter a race, regular exercise increases your staying power, helps you manage your weight, and contributes to a longer, disease-free life.

It doesn't take a rigorous, highly structured regimen to enjoy the physical benefits of exercise. Something as easy as walking for thirty minutes four times a week will pay off. If you or your institution has the means, you can even invest in a treadmill equipped with a workstation so you can exercise while at the office.

Your family and social life can be enhanced through exercise as well. Take a walk or a bike ride with your spouse, kids, or a group of friends. Join a running club. Most running clubs will match you with a group of folks who have similar goals and fitness levels.

Eat Well. For a person with no underlying or known medical conditions, the Mayo Clinic recommends a diet in which 45–65 percent of caloric intake comes from carbohydrates, with an emphasis on fruits and vegetables; 10–35 percent from protein; and 20–35 percent from fats, with an emphasis on unsaturated fats.

As already mentioned, carbohydrates are found in fruits and vegetables, but you can also find them in rice, pasta and whole grains. To my delight, even dark chocolate is a source of carbohydrates, though I would use that one in moderation because it is a refined carbohydrate. Refined carbohydrates are those that have been processed to improve their shelf-life and/or taste, but in going through the transformation, important nutrients like fiber and water have been removed from the food. Therefore, it is better to eat brown rice in place of white rice, and 100 percent whole wheat bread instead of white bread.

Proteins are found in meats, poultry, and fish, though most authorities suggest that if you eat meat, you stick with the leaner cuts such as sirloin. Legumes are also a good source of protein for those who wish to minimize their consumption of animal products.

Fat is important since it is a source of stored energy and helps food taste better. However, the fats in our diet should be unsaturated, not saturated or trans fats. Saturated fats are the liquids we find in the pan after we fry bacon or roast a chicken, and trans facts are typically manufactured fats. Saturated fats and trans fats are solids at room temperature. Unsaturated fats, the good fats, are found in olive oil, vegetable oil, and fish oils. They stay in their liquid form when cooled to room temperature.

Here are some other tips for eating well.

> Unless you are in training for a big athletic event, keep caloric intake to no more than 2,000 calories a day. According to LiveStrong.com, "A diet of 2,000 calories a day is reasonable and can easily accommodate all your nutritional needs if you plan your meals correctly."

> Stay away from soda and even some energy drinks. Most are full of sugar and caffeine. Check the labels.

> Minimize your intake of processed foods. The closer your nutrients are to their natural state, the better. In other words, choose raw vegetables over potato chips, and eat strawberries for dessert instead of chocolate cake.

> Drink lots of water. Staying hydrated is important for maintaining focus and preventing mood swings.

> Consume alcohol moderately or avoid it.

Eat for Energy Management. In his book *The Corporate Athlete*, Jack Groppel, Ph.D., likens the physical and mental stresses of a business executive to those of a professional athlete and says, "Nutrition may well be the single most important limiting factor preventing Corporate Athletes from achieving their maximum potential." Since athletes excel at eating for energy management, I think we can learn a lesson or two from them.

Their regimen for staying in an optimum energy zone (figure 10) involves eating three traditional but reduced-calorie meals per day along with a midday and an afternoon snack. The snacks will replace the reduction in calories in your meals and will prevent your energy levels from spiking and crashing. In other words, you'll stay on an even keel and avoid the midmorning or mid-afternoon blues and lack of concentration.

Figure 10: Dividing Food Intake to Maintain the Optimum Energy Zone

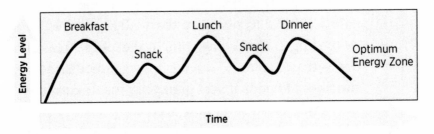

According to the U.S. Department of Agriculture (USDA), the following is an example of a menu that will keep you energized and focused throughout the day.

Breakfast
Cold cereal:
> *1 cup ready-to-eat oat cereal*
> *1 medium banana*
> *½ cup fat-free milk*

1 slice whole wheat toast
 1 tsp. tub margarine
Beverage: 1 cup prune juice

Mid-morning Snack
 ¼ cup dried apricots

Lunch
Tuna salad sandwich:
 2 slices rye bread
 2 ounces tuna
 1 tbsp. mayonnaise
 1 tbsp. chopped celery
 ½ cup shredded lettuce
1 medium peach
Beverage: 1 cup fat-free milk

Afternoon Snack
1 cup flavored yogurt (chocolate)

Dinner
Roasted chicken:
 3 ounces cooked chicken breast
1 large sweet potato, roasted
½ cup succotash (limas & corn)
 1 tsp. tub margarine
1 ounce whole wheat roll
 1 tsp. tub margarine
Beverage: 1 cup water or 1 cup unsweetened coffee or tea without creamer or whitener

This is just an example of a 2,000-calorie menu for a single day. Depending on your age, gender, activity level, and weight goals, you will want to consider increasing or decreasing the total number of calories you consume. Other sample menus from the USDA can be found at myplate.gov.

Don't Smoke

> *"That's all I have to say about that."*
> —Forrest Gump

What Are the Steps to Attaining a Balanced Life?

Attaining balance in your life starts by taking a step back and deciding what is important to you, what your personal values are, and how they are positioned in relation to your personal and professional goals. We all have a set of values that, over time, have become ingrained in us. Understanding your values, examining them, and then making sure those values are aligned with your goals will assist you in keeping your life in balance.

In addition, think about your passions. What makes you want to get out of bed every morning? What energizes you? What grabs your attention or gets your heart beating a little faster? Then consider which area of your life will allow you to experience those passions. Is it your career, your personal time, or the moments spent with your family? All three would be ideal. Let's discuss how to maintain a balanced life while achieving the lofty goals I'm sure you have set for your business.

Build Downtime into Your Schedule. Think about your cell phone for a moment. Doesn't it periodically need to be recharged? If you use it frequently, you may even need to recharge it every day. Your mind and body are just like your phone; they need regular recharging too. Building time into your schedule to do something you enjoy will let you recharge. Never forget that a little relaxation goes a long way.

Drop Activities that Zap Your Time and Energy. Examine all your activities and drop those that are not in line with your current values or goals or don't move you towards the life you have envisioned. For example, when it comes to community outreach, make sure you are involved with a cause about which you are passionate. Don't let your ego get in the way here. Just because someone asks you to serve on a board or committee doesn't mean you should. While it is flattering to be asked, the prudent course may be to respectfully decline.

Manage Your Stress. It's hard to feel as if your life is in balance when you are constantly stressed. However, the goal is not to completely eliminate stress from your life, but to manage it. In fact, some stress, like preparing for a presentation, can be good for you. Here are five tips for managing stress.

Expect the unexpected. Learn to go with the flow. Issues will pop up every day. You know that, so don't let them derail you from the task at hand. Either deal with them as quickly and efficiently as possible, delegate the issues, or forget about them until later or forget about them all together.

Understand and then manage your priorities. Every day, as you are getting ready to leave the office, make a list of the things you need to accomplish the next day. Then prioritize that list. Leave it in the middle of your desk so that when you arrive the next morning, you know exactly what your priorities are for the day. This knowledge jumpstarts your day and eliminates the need to take the first thirty to forty-five minutes to figure out where you are headed. Then, make sure you and your team have a laser-like focus on what is needed to achieve your goals.

Don't be afraid to delegate. While others might not do some tasks the same way as you or as well as you, you still need to think about letting go. The people you reluctantly entrust with assignments might just surprise you with how well they execute their undertakings. When you do delegate, make sure the individuals understand their mission and are prepared. You may have to walk them through the steps the first couple of times before you turn them loose.

Minimize procrastination. Do important tasks now; don't wait. The anxiety created by waiting mentally distracts you and doesn't accomplish anything.

Have quiet time. This is time to think, meditate or pray.

Maintain a Positive Attitude. Cultivate an optimistic approach to your life and your business. Things will not always go your way—there will be setbacks—but maintaining a positive attitude is more about how you react to these bumps in the road than the bumps themselves.

Summary
In varying ways, we are all out of balance over the course of a year, a decade, and a lifetime. The degree of balance in our lives will ebb and flow like the currents of the ocean. Maintaining optimum health and tranquility is a lifelong endeavor, but the tips provided in this chapter will help you improve your ability to operate in a balanced zone.

Enjoy the life you are building!

➤ Action Plan

1. Start an exercise plan.

2. Develop your first week's meal plan.

3. Align your goals with your values.

ACKNOWLEDGMENTS

SOME FRIENDSHIPS HAVE A WAY of coming and going while others endure the ups and downs of life. This book would not have been possible without two such enduring friendships, those of Ralph Sharp and Ron George. Both relationships started on a professional level but grew to a point of personal friendship and respect.

I met Ralph Sharp at a company dinner as he regaled the table with his military stories. I immediately took a liking to him, and our friendship has grown over the years. I began working with Ralph when he was an advisor and a top club producer in a credit union program in Texas. Later, when he was a sales manager in Florida, we would travel together working with advisors in the bank channel he managed. Our mission was to increase the overall sales of the territory and catch a baseball game or two if teams happened to be in spring training. Many of the ideas and techniques shared in this book were developed during our drives together across Alligator Alley in southern Florida.

After a long and successful career as an advisor and sales manager with New York Life, Ron George decided it was time for a change. He became a sales manager for a group of investment advisors in financial institutions throughout the southeastern United States. In time, my office door and Ron's ended up side by side. In the days, months, and years that followed,

Ron became not only a friend but a mentor. He has assisted me by sharing his experiences and wisdom on several occasions. Many of his opinions, thoughts, and convictions are found in the pages of this book.

Finally, I'd like to acknowledge my best friend, my wife, Marcia. She is one of the wisest individuals I know. I respect her opinion and ask for it often. She is always able to patiently help me muddle through my thoughts until I come to a clear solution.

Gary Weuve

BIBLIOGRAPHY

Beckwith, Harry. *What Clients Love: A Field Guide to Growing Your Business*. New York: Warner Business Books, 2003.

Collins, Jim. *Good to Great: Why Some Companies Make the Leap... and Others Don't*. New York: HarperCollins Publishers, Inc., 2001.

Covey, Stephen R. *The 7 Habits of Highly Effective People: Powerful Lessons in Personal Change*. New York: Free Press, 2004.

Covey, Stephen M. R. *The Speed of Trust: The One Thing That Changes Everything*. New York: Free Press, 2006.

Gerber, Michael E. *The E-Myth Revisited*. New York: HarperCollins Publishers, Inc., 2001.

Gladwell, Malcolm. *The Tipping Point: How Little Things Can Make a Big Difference*. New York: Little, Brown and Company, 2000.

Groppel, Jack and Bob Andelman. *The Corporate Athlete: How to Achieve Maximal Performance in Business and Life*. New York: John C. Wiley and Sons, Inc., 2000.

LiveStrong.com. "Recommended 2,000-Calorie Diet." Beverly Bird. Last modified October 15, 2010. http://www.livestrong.com/article/280254-recommended-2-000-calorie-diet/.

Maister, David H., Charles H. Green, and Robert M. Galford. *The Trusted Advisor.* New York: Touchstone, 2000.

Mayo Clinic. "Healthy Diet: End the Guesswork with These Nutrition Guidelines." Mayo Clinic Staff. Last modified February 22, 2011. http://www.mayoclinic.com/health/healthy-diet/NU00200.

Montoya, Peter. *The Brand Called You.* New York: The McGraw-Hill Companies, 2009.

O'Brien,Timothy P. *The Power of Personal Branding: Creating Celebrity Status with Your Target Audience.* Mendham, NJ: Mendham Publishing, 2007.

Rowland, Mary. *Best Practices of Financial Advisors.* Princeton, New Jersey: Bloomberg Press, 1997.

United States Department of Agriculture. "Sample Menus for a 2000 Calorie Food Pattern." Last modified March 2011. http://www.choosemyplate.gov/food-groups/downloads/Sample_Menus-2000Cals-DG2010.pdf.

West, Scott and Mitch Anthony. *Storyselling for Financial Advisors: How Top Producers Sell.* Chicago: Dearborn Financial Publishing, Inc., 2000.

CPSIA information can be obtained at www.ICGtesting.com
Printed in the USA
LVOW06*0400290814

401408LV00002B/2/P